THE WHISPER OF
GOD

The Whisper of God
Written by Allison T. Cain
Edited by Jeannie Norris
Cover Design by Kent Swecker
Family Photograph by Ashley Crutchfield

Allison T. Cain
[atcain2@earthlink.net]

FIRST PRINTING

ISBN: 1450514863
EAN-13: 9781450514866

Printed in the United States of America

THE WHISPER OF
GOD

Allison T. Cain

THE WHISPER OF GOD

A 52-week devotional to take you through the year & encourage you to see God in the ordinary.

Written by: Allison T. Cain

Edited by Jeannie Norris

Cover Design by Kent Swecker

Family Photograph by Ashley Crutchfield

The LORD said,
"Go out and stand on the mountain
in the presence of the LORD,
for the LORD is about to pass by."
Then a great and powerful wind tore the mountains apart
and shattered the rocks before the LORD,
but the LORD was not in the wind.
After the wind there was an earthquake,
but the LORD was not in the earthquake.
After the earthquake came a fire,
but the LORD was not in the fire.
And after the fire came a gentle whisper.

— 1 Kings 19:11-12

"Love your divine devotions and the scriptures and the way you have set it up so that you can really "dwell' over it and have it really sink in and make a difference in your life. THANK YOU!" *Mitzi Melton*

"Did you write this just for me?" *Laura Barbee*

"We really do enjoy your devotional. It's really neat 'cause we have the chance to experience a bit of who you are through the devotion. It also encourages us to know that every Christian faces some of the same struggles and we're not alone." *Eric & Mimi McMillian*

"Allison's writing challenges me to be still and listen to hear from God; to be aware of his presence in the midst of the busyness of life." *Jennifer Crawford*

"Your words and perspective are such an inspiration and will touch so many lives. Everyone that reads your messages will blessed by your wisdom and reap the rewards of your obedience and devotion to our Heavenly Father. Thank you for answering His call to service that was placed on your heart." *Kelly Sokolowski*

"Your devotional book could not have landed in my in-box at a better time. I love what you've written! You've done a beautiful job... and helped me when I needed help." *Jeannie Norris*

"Beautiful. Really." *Jeanne Wittig*

For my Heavenly Father, who never gave up on me and continued to pursue me until He had my WHOLE heart.

🌟

THE WHISPER OF GOD

www.thewhisperofgod.wordpress.com
Devotions that encourage you to see God in the *ordinary*.

✶✶

"Let us be silent, so that we may hear the whisper of God."
— Ralph Waldo Emerson

Introduction

Several years ago, I started writing down all the amazing ways God used my day-to-day activities, children, family, friends and nature to teach me. The more I wrote, the more I noticed God in my daily life. It became an exercise of the heart and grew my relationship with Christ in a way I had never experienced. I began to hear God whisper to my heart His desires and lessons for me. I hope that reading some of my stories will encourage you to stop and listen for His whisper in *your* life!

As you go through the year, it is my prayer that you will discover two things.

1. God is at work in your everyday life. The closer you grow in your relationship with Him, the more you will see Him. The more you see Him, the more you desire to know Him. Whatever way it happens for you, I pray it happens.

2. Discover the value of reading the Bible. God wants to communicate with you and He uses His Word (the Bible) to do so. I hope you discover that by dwelling on His Word, He will reveal the desires of His heart to you.

One more thing

Take your time. We never do that these days. Read just one a week, sit on the scriptures in the devotion, think about them, reflect and listen. I pray God does some amazing things in your life and in your relationship with Him as you take this journey.

How to use this devotional

There are 52 devotions, one for each week of the year. Try not to move ahead, but to savor and reflect on God's Word for the entire week. After each devotion, there is a section for you to write down your thoughts and revelations. I hope this will help you discover what God is whispering to you. The format is simple. I call them the 5 R's.

Relate – How does this message relate to your life?

Reread – Read the scriptures throughout today's message each day of this week.

Revealed – Did God reveal anything new to you as you reread the scriptures? God might not reveal to you today but tomorrow; maybe not this week, but the next. Don't give up.

Respond – We are accountable for our actions and thoughts. Think about your week. Are you on the right track with God, your family, your children, your life, etc.? If not, what changes do you feel you need to make?

Reflect – Write down any other thoughts that you had. Do this throughout the week because you may not have any thoughts when you first read a devotion. However, you may wake up in the middle of the night with a word from God you can't ignore.

All scriptures are noted in bold and in the NIV translation unless otherwise noted.

WEEK 1 ~ GOD DOESN'T YELL

Scripture: 1 King 19:11-12

We have a God who forgives, encourages, restores, loves, inspires and whispers. Yes, whispers! I am sure there have been days that my children wish I was more like God. No yelling! More whispering!

"Let us be silent that we may hear the whisper of God." —— Ralph Waldo Emerson

I love this quote. I had it above the tub in our last house. What better place to be still and quiet, right?! It is such a great reminder of how God speaks to us. But we have to learn to slow down, reflect and listen to His whispers throughout the day – not just when we are in the bathtub.

I believe that, if we go long enough without listening to God and taking time to hear His whispers, He will make the time *for us*. Over a year ago I experienced a scary medical ordeal. I was convinced that God was using this "fieldtrip" to reinforce the fact that I had been doing too much and not turning to Him as I should. I was taking on more and more without considering if these were tasks that God desired for me. I joked about this to a friend visiting me in the hospital. I told her that I had not signed the permission slip to go on this trip and I was ready for things to return to normal. She quickly reminded me that God does not need our permission. He just acts!

How true! More than anything, God desires for us to seek Him. My friend once said, "It's not a religion! It's a relationship!" Oh, how God longs for a relationship with us. He does not care where we have been, what we have done, how we acted in that situation - He accepts us for what we have been, washes our souls, restores us to who He created us to be – and we get to start all over. A clean slate. Oh, how I love our God.

The LORD said, "Go out and stand on the mountain in the presence of the LORD, for the LORD is about to pass by." Then a great and powerful wind tore the mountains apart and shattered the rocks before the LORD, but the LORD was not in the wind. After the wind there was an earthquake, but the LORD was not in the earthquake. After the earthquake came a fire, but the LORD was not in the fire. And after the fire came a gentle whisper. — 1 King 19:11-12

So, I have tried to slow down and listen to God's whispers. The lessons and advice He wants my soul and heart to hear. I pray that I can keep this perspective because I don't want to take another fieldtrip and learn the hard way again! Can you hear God whispering? How do you want to learn?

Relate – Can you relate to the message or theme? How? _____

_____

_____

_____

_____

_____

_____

Reread – Read the scriptures throughout today's message again.

_____

Revealed – Did God reveal anything new to you? Don't forget to come back and read them daily this week. God might not reveal to you today, but tomorrow.

_____

_____

_____

_____

_____

_____

Respond – Think about your week. Has God been whispering?

_____

_____

_____

_____

_____

_____

Reflect – Any other thoughts?

_____

_____

_____

_____

_____

_____

WEEK 2 ~ PITY PARTY

Scriptures: James 5:7-8, Hebrews 6:12

It was one of those days. I was hosting a private pity party for myself. Everything going on around me seemed to catch up, and I was feeling overwhelmed and useless. I decided that I deserved this time to pout and it was OK to have a pity party for myself as long as I didn't stay at the party for more than a few days. Have you ever had a time that that?

Be patient, then, brothers, until the Lord's coming. See how the farmer waits for the land to yield its valuable crop and how patient he is for the autumn and spring rains. You too, be patient and stand firm, because the Lord's coming is near. — James 5:7-8

As I was driving my two children back from Vacation Bible School, they began discussing what they were going to be when they grew up. All of a sudden my youngest (almost 3 at the time) piped up and asked me, "Mommy, what are you going to be when you grow up?"

After a moment of silence and trying to decide whether or not to explain I was already grown up, I went for it. "Well, that is a great question," I told him, thinking if I don't know by now, I am probably in trouble.

"How about Supergirl?" my son chimed in. "OK, sure" (as I thought to myself — I do try to be Superhero every day. That sounds like a reasonable thing.). So I agreed, "Yes, I will be Supergirl when I grow up."

"OK, good" he said. "How about tomorrow?" "Tomorrow?" I asked. "Yes, why don't you grow up tomorrow?" he repeated. WOW! Talk about words straight from God. My son was right. It was time for me to grow up, take hold of God's Word and leave my pity party behind!

I began to think about how often God has spoken to me through my children, friends and family. Have you ever felt like God was speaking to you through someone else, their words or actions?

We do not want you to become lazy, but to imitate those who through faith and patience inherit what has been promised. — Hebrews 6:12

I also began to think about how many times I had missed what God was trying to show or tell me because I was too busy, too distracted or too content to wallow around in self-pity. We need to take hold of God's promises and trust that our Father in Heaven is all we need, and He will provide and love us!

Relate – Can you relate to the message or theme? How? _____

_____

_____

_____

_____

_____

Reread – Read the scriptures throughout today's message again.

_____

Revealed – Did God reveal anything new to you? Don't forget to come back and read them daily this week. God might not reveal to you today, but tomorrow.

_____

_____

_____

_____

_____

_____

Respond – Think about your week. Has God been whispering?

_____

_____

_____

_____

_____

_____

Reflect – Any other thoughts?

_____

_____

_____

_____

_____

_____

WEEK 3 ~ WATERS OF LIFE

Scriptures: Jeremiah 29:11, Proverbs 3:5-6

We had just spent the most amazing week in the NC mountains. It was such a welcome treat to get away from the heat, hustle and house building in Raleigh. The cabin we stayed in was on 25 beautiful acres. Big Horse Creek ran right through the property. The sound of the water rushing through the rocks was mesmerizing. I would wade out to the center of the creek to sit on this huge rock. It was so big that it had created a fork in the creek, and water rushed by it on both sides. It is amazing how the years of water have molded, shaped and changed the rocks in the creek. They are all so unique in color, shape, texture and size.

It reminded me of how we all start out as one person and, as we go through the waters (many times, rapids) of life, we are molded and changed like the rocks. I had just turned 36, and I'd like to think that I am a much better person than I was 15 years ago. I have experienced so many joyful times, but I've also felt the crushing blow of losing a friend to cancer and other very difficult times. Times when the waters of life seemed they might carry me away, but I've held firm in my trust of the Lord even though I don't pretend to understand His plan! There are so many things that don't make sense to me, and I can't comprehend how they could be part of God's plan. I just remain faithful and know that God keeps all His promises and His plan is perfect.

For I know the plans I have for you, declares the LORD, plans to prosper you and not to harm you, plans to give you hope and a future. —Jeremiah 29:11

I kept a small stone from the creek to remind me that being molded, shaped and refined through the waters of life can make me a more beautiful woman, wife, mother and follower of Jesus Christ.

**Trust in the LORD with all your heart
and lean not on your own understanding;
in all your ways acknowledge him,
and he will make your paths straight.
— Proverbs 3:5-6**

Relate – Can you relate to the message or theme? How? _____

_____

_____

_____

_____

_____

_____

Reread – Read the scriptures throughout today's message again.

_____

Revealed – Did God reveal anything new to you? Don't forget to come back and read them daily this week. God might not reveal to you today, but tomorrow.

_____

_____

_____

_____

_____

_____

Respond – Think about your week. Has God been whispering?

_____

_____

_____

_____

_____

_____

Reflect – Any other thoughts?

_____

_____

_____

_____

_____

_____

WEEK 4 ~ ALL THE MONEY IN THE WORLD

Scriptures: Ephesians 1:7, Acts 26:18

I can't believe how fast time moves when you are watching your kids grow up. When my son turned 4, his birthday recently brought to mind one of my favorite things he said when he was just 2 years old.

It was just another day of running errands and trying to get everything checked off the to-do list. As we pulled into the parking lot of the bank, my son asked, "Mommy, where are we?" My then 4-year-old daughter interrupted before I could answer and said, "This is where we put all our money so we can save it to give to God to pay for our sins."

Oh, I had to chuckle. How adorable, I thought! Then, I realized how scary that would be. I'm not sure how much money I would need to pay for my sins, but I am quite sure that we have nowhere near enough in our bank account! In fact, all the money in the world probably would not cover it! I stopped at that moment and said a prayer of thanksgiving. How grateful I am that God sent His only Son to die for me. How grateful and how unbelievable!

In him we have redemption through his blood, the forgiveness of sins, in accordance with the riches of God's grace.
— Ephesians 1:7

No money, no kind deed, no donation, no gift nor speech needed! Just a confession of our sins to our Father in Heaven. It almost sounds too easy doesn't it? I think that is why it takes longer for us to forgive ourselves. Why we all feel the guilt linger. It can linger for days, weeks, months or even years. It is why some turn to drugs, alcohol, shopping or other distractions. Sometimes it is difficult to trust that we are forgiven.

[T]o open their eyes and turn them from darkness to light, and from the power of Satan to God, so that they may receive forgiveness of sins and a place among those who are sanctified by faith in me.
— Acts 26:18

Relate – Can you relate to the message or theme? How? _____

_____

_____

_____

_____

_____

_____

Reread – Read the scriptures throughout today's message again.

_____

Revealed – Did God reveal anything new to you? Don't forget to come back and read them daily this week. God might not reveal to you today, but tomorrow.

_____

_____

_____

_____

_____

_____

Respond – Think about your week. Has God been whispering?

_____

_____

_____

_____

_____

_____

Reflect – Any other thoughts?

_____

_____

_____

_____

_____

_____

WEEK 5 ~ FORGIVENESS

Scriptures: Micah 7:18, 1 Corinthians 10:23-24

During a rushed Monday morning trying to get everyone out the door, I lost my patience with the kids and yelled at them to please hurry and put their shoes – for the fourth time.

Later that morning, before we went into the grocery store, I asked my son to crawl in my lap. As I hugged him I told him I was sorry I had lost my temper. I explained that I was in a hurry and frustrated, but I still should not have yelled at him. He embraced me and said, "I love it when you say that, Mommy."

After this moment, we climbed out of the car and a man who had been sweeping in front of his store said, "Excuse me, but I just have to tell you that was a Kodak moment. I don't know what you two were talking about, but I have never seen a look of such contentment on a little boy's face as I just did on your son's."

Wow! What a powerful confirmation that asking forgiveness and being forgiven is such an important part of our existence – our happy existence. Can you imagine God's look of total contentment with us when we acknowledge our sin and we ask Him for forgiveness?

Who is a God like you, who pardons sin and forgives the transgression of the remnant of his inheritance? You do not stay angry forever but delight to show mercy. —Micah 7:18

Why is it so difficult for us to ask for forgiveness? Why is it so difficult to forgive others after they have hurt us so deeply? It is pride, disappointment, anger, bitterness?

Oh, how I wish I could say I had perfected these skills. I know I can only do these things because of the strength, courage and love that Christ has given me. I pray we all learn how to love more, forgive quickly and extend grace freely like children do and our Father in Heaven has and always will with perfection!

Looking at it one way, you could say, "Anything goes. Because of God's immense generosity and grace, we don't have to dissect and scrutinize every action to see if it will pass muster." But the point is not to just get by. We want to live well, but our foremost efforts should be to help others live well. — 1 Corinthians 10:23-24, The Message

Relate – Can you relate to the message or theme? How? _____

_____

_____

_____

_____

_____

_____

Reread – Read the scriptures throughout today's message again.

_____

Revealed – Did God reveal anything new to you? Don't forget to come back and read them daily this week. God might not reveal to you today, but tomorrow.

_____

_____

_____

_____

_____

_____

Respond – Think about your week. Has God been whispering?

_____

_____

_____

_____

_____

_____

Reflect – Any other thoughts?

_____

_____

_____

_____

_____

_____

WEEK 6 ~ MAY I TAKE YOUR ORDER?

Scriptures: Psalm 139, Isaiah 25:1

It had been a long morning, and I just wanted to go home and take a nap. I told my daughter on the way home from running errands that I would like to order a thunderstorm for the afternoon because that would be great "nap-taking weather." She replies, "But Mommy, it's not a restaurant you can order from. It's God's thunderstorm. He will send it if He wants to."

I am certainly guilty of "placing my order" with God instead of prayerfully seeking Him, giving Him control and trusting in His perfect plan. I have learned the hard way more times than I would like to admit. Although I still falter, I am so much better at listening and learning from God. I have a strong desire to seek God's path for my life. I don't always understand it, I don't always like it and sometimes He certainly thinks more highly of me than I do of myself. It takes a lot of trust and a lot of faith.

It is so difficult to fathom that God has had a plan, His perfect plan, for me since before he knit me in my mother's womb. In reality, He knows me better than I will ever know myself. Read a little bit of **Psalm 139**.

O LORD, you have searched me
and you know me.
You know when I sit and when I rise;
you perceive my thoughts from afar.
You discern my going out and my lying down;
you are familiar with all my ways.
Before a word is on my tongue
you know it completely, O LORD.
You hem me in—behind and before;
you have laid your hand upon me.
Such knowledge is too wonderful for me,
too lofty for me to attain.

Once again, God spoke to me through my children. The little ones He knit into my womb. I am always amazed at how small children can make such a simple statement and have such a great impact on me. I pray that one day my children will read these stories and understand what an impact they have made on me and my walk with God.

O LORD, you are my God; I will exalt you and praise your name, for in perfect faithfulness you have done marvelous things, things planned long ago. — Isaiah 25:1

Relate – Can you relate to the message or theme? How? _____

_____

_____

_____

_____

_____

_____

Reread – Read the scriptures throughout today's message again.

_____

Revealed – Did God reveal anything new to you? Don't forget to come back and read them daily this week. God might not reveal to you today, but tomorrow.

_____

_____

_____

_____

_____

_____

Respond – Think about your week. Has God been whispering?

_____

_____

_____

_____

_____

_____

Reflect – Any other thoughts?

_____

_____

_____

_____

_____

_____

WEEK 7 ~ GNATS!

Scriptures: Isaiah 26:3, Numbers 6:25-26

You will keep in perfect peace all who trust in you, all whose thoughts are fixed on you!
— Isaiah 26:3

Yes, gnats! Those pesky little flies that love to hang around in the summertime. I was soaking in some morning sunshine and savoring a little quiet time for my Bible study. Sitting right on the beach overlooking the water – the setting could not have been more perfect – except for the gnats!

They were swarming around me. In my hair, my ears, my mouth. It was horrible. I knew this wasn't an accident. The Deceiver would love nothing more than for me to stop studying God's Word. He will even use the smallest of insects to accomplish his goal. Well, I gave up on the perfect scenery and went inside, but kept studying!

I couldn't help but think of all the other little things in my life that distract me and keep me from studying God's Word, taking time to pray and listening for God's whisper. There are certainly more things to distract me from God than there are things that lead me closer to Him. Especially in the world we live in.

A few years ago, "fitting" God in was a challenge, but the more I did it the more I noticed all the time I had. Granted, I had been spending it in other ways and I have learned to fill it with God – not TV, not talking on the phone, not reading the latest gossip magazine while getting a pedicure. A little like spending all that time untangling my son's Spiderman fishing pole. Not what I wanted to do at first and VERY challenging, but after seeing his face light up when I fixed it – that was worth all the time in the world. We need to get untangled and stop wasting our time on things of this world!

We need to sort through the things that take up more time than God.

I believe that this is one of those skills we will never master. We will always need God's help to stay focused on Him and not the things of this world. I certainly have no power or discipline to do this on my own. It all comes from Him!

[T]he LORD make his face shine upon you and be gracious to you; the LORD turn his face toward you and give you peace.
— Numbers 6:25-26

Relate – Can you relate to the message or theme? How? _____

_____

_____

_____

_____

_____

_____

Reread – Read the scriptures throughout today's message again.

_____

Revealed – Did God reveal anything new to you? Don't forget to come back and read them daily this week. God might not reveal to you today, but tomorrow.

_____

_____

_____

_____

_____

_____

Respond – Think about your week. Has God been whispering?

_____

_____

_____

_____

_____

_____

Reflect – Any other thoughts?

_____

_____

_____

_____

_____

WEEK 8 ~ "SAVER"

Scriptures: Psalm 25:5, Ephesians 5:8 & 10

It had been a particularly tough day. As I was saying prayers with the kids before bed my eyes welled up with tears. I had to pause for a moment to collect myself. My son looked up at me and wiped a tear off my cheek. He said, "Don't worry Mommy. I'll be your saver." What a great little superhero!

I wonder how many times my Father in Heaven whispered to me, "I'll be your SAVIOR," as He counted the tears that fell from my face, walked beside me during a time of sin or difficulty. I'm so thankful He never gave up on me and kept nudging my heart back to Him. He chased after my heart for many years before I was finally able to understand what it really meant to have Him in my life and accept all He was offering me. For so long, it was hard to comprehend how I could be worthy of His unconditional love, total forgiveness, grace, acceptance and mercy. The truth is I'm not worthy of it! None of us are, but God gives it to us anyway.

[G]uide me in your truth and teach me, for you are God my Savior, and my hope is in you all day long. Psalm 25:5

Kay Arthur recapped Ephesians this way in one of her books: "When we are saved, each of us becomes a member of Christ's body, forged with resurrection power, and seated with Him in heavenly places above all rule, power, and authority. Nothing can alter our position. It is set forever in heaven. But position is one thing; living accordingly is another."

For so many years of my life I held the position but did not live like I did! I am learning to own my mistakes and my past. I don't need to be ashamed, but instead ask forgiveness and move forward to living a life that is pleasing to God. Giving up my "old self" and walking in the light.

[F]or you were formerly darkness, but now you are light in the Lord; walk as children of light trying to learn what is pleasing to the Lord. Ephesians 5:8 & 10

I thank God that He allows me a fresh start every day! Another chance to do the right thing because there are many days when it feels I have failed miserably at pleasing Him. I praise Him for His abundant love, forgiveness and grace.

Relate – Can you relate to the message or theme? How? _____

_____

_____

_____

_____

_____

Reread – Read the scriptures throughout today's message again.

_____

Revealed – Did God reveal anything new to you? Don't forget to come back and read them daily this week. God might not reveal to you today, but tomorrow.

_____

_____

_____

_____

_____

_____

Respond – Think about your week. Has God been whispering?

_____

_____

_____

_____

_____

Reflect – Any other thoughts?

_____

_____

_____

_____

_____

WEEK 9 ~ ONE MORE THOUGHT – "SAVER"

Scriptures: Exodus 20:3, Psalm 42:11, Romans 8:38-39

In my last devotion, I told the story of how my son wiped away a tear when I was crying and told me not to worry – that he would be my "saver." I realized there was another lesson in this story. So many times I think we try to make a friend, spouse, parent or family member our "saver" instead of our one and only Savior, Jesus Christ. We are setting a course for disaster when we do this.

First, it is a sin to put any other before our Lord and Savior. It is the first of the Ten Commandments even before thou shall not murder, steal or commit adultery. **You shall have no other gods before me. Exodus 20:3** The fact that God put this commandment above all the others should speak volumes to us. I believe if we would just follow this first commandment, all the others would never be a problem because as we move closer to Christ we desire to live more as He did.

Secondly, no one has the ability to give us unconditional love, grace, mercy, forgiveness; cleanse us of our sins; and promise us eternal life except our Heavenly Father. He alone can give us those things.

Thirdly, we are setting up ourselves – and those in our lives we have placed in the "saver" role – for a tremendous failure and disappointment. It can cause great hardship in the relationship and oftentimes will end it.

Why are you downcast, O my soul? Why so disturbed within me? Put your hope in God, for I will yet praise him, my Savior and my God. Psalm 42:11

Let me be clear, I don't think we elevate people to this level on purpose or with intention. I think it just happens over time. We begin to rely on the individual more than we do on God, and this allows sin into our lives.

The great news is that we can repent of this sin and start over with God. He is always there. Nothing can separate us from Him. We only need to claim His promises and accept His love.

For I am convinced that neither death, nor life, nor angels, nor principalities, nor things present, nor things to come, nor powers, nor height, nor depth, nor any other created thing, shall be able to separate us from the love of God, which is in Christ Jesus our Lord. Romans 8:38-39

Relate – Can you relate to the message or theme? How? _____

_____

_____

_____

_____

_____

_____

Reread – Read the scriptures throughout today's message again.

_____

Revealed – Did God reveal anything new to you? Don't forget to come back and read them daily this week. God might not reveal to you today, but tomorrow.

_____

_____

_____

_____

_____

_____

Respond – Think about your week. Has God been whispering?

_____

_____

_____

_____

_____

_____

Reflect – Any other thoughts?

_____

_____

_____

_____

_____

_____

WEEK 10 ~ SHE'S HAVING A MOMENT

Scriptures: James 1:5, 1 John 5:14-15, Psalm 145:18

We were at the mall one day before my daughter started kindergarten. It was time to eat and she wanted to choose the lunch destination. I was busy trying to explain to her that she got new earrings, so her brother got to choose where we would eat lunch. As you can imagine, that wasn't going over so well. As I crouched down in the middle of the mall trying to work through the tears and drama, some men passed by. I politely said, "Please excuse us. We are having a moment." My son speaks up and yells above the crying, "YEAH! She is having a moment!"

Later that evening, when I actually had time to think, I had to laugh. I wonder how many times God says that about me? "Oh, she is having a moment!"

If you need wisdom, ask our generous God, and he will give it to you. He will not rebuke you for asking. James 1:5

I often find myself caught up in a situation, problem or concern that I am "having a moment" about and realize that I haven't taken it to God. I have to remind myself to stop and go to God in prayer to seek His wisdom, peace and guidance. I would love to be able to say I always realize this right away, but sometimes it's days before I remember to give it to God. The BIG stuff is easier to remember. You know things like job loss, finances, health concerns, etc. The big issues of life are always on the surface. It is the small things that can get pushed to the back of my mind and nag away at my thoughts.

God cares about all things. The request may seem small or of little concern compared to the long list of major prayer requests you have. But as long as it is important to us, it is important to God. We can take the smallest concern or petition and place it at His feet.

And this is the confidence that we have toward him, that if we ask anything according to his will he hears us. And if we know that he hears us in whatever we ask, we know that we have the requests that we have asked of him. 1 John 5:14-15

The next time you find yourself "having a moment," stop and give it to God. Pray boldly and confidently. Trust God to hear your prayers. Take time to be still and listen for His answer!

The LORD is near to all who call on him, to all who call on him in truth. Psalm 145:18

Relate – Can you relate to the message or theme? How? _____

_____

_____

_____

_____

_____

_____

Reread – Read the scriptures throughout today's message again.

_____

Revealed – Did God reveal anything new to you? Don't forget to come back and read them daily this week. God might not reveal to you today, but tomorrow.

_____

_____

_____

_____

_____

_____

Respond – Think about your week. Has God been whispering?

_____

_____

_____

_____

_____

_____

Reflect – Any other thoughts?

_____

_____

_____

_____

_____

_____

WEEK 11 ~ CONVICTED

Scriptures: Mark 8:36, John 15:4

One of my favorite songs is *Lose My Soul* by Toby Mac. Some of the lyrics are below:

Father God, I am clay in your hands,
Help me to stay that way through all life's demands,
'Cause they chip and they nag and they pull at me,
And every little thing I make up my mind to be,

**

Everything that I see draws me,
Though it's only in You that I can truly see that it's a feast for the eyes — a low blow to purpose.
And I'm a little kid at a three ring circus.

**

I don't want to gain the whole world, and lose my soul,
Don't wanna walk away, let me hear the people say.

That song is based on **Mark 8:36**. It says, **What good is it for a man to gain the whole world, yet forfeit his soul?**

In this self-absorbed and wicked world we live in, there are many things to attract our attention away from God. If we don't take a proactive approach to studying God's Word, seeking Him daily in prayer and growing our relationship with Him, we may gain the whole world but, as the scripture says, we will forfeit our soul.

I walked around for years calling myself a Christian not realizing that I was nothing more than a casual Christian — a hypocrite, really. I shudder to think of all the things I said and did during this time. I am sure my actions did NOTHING to bring others to know Christ. It took me many years to realize that what I had was religion, not a relationship. It is a relationship with Christ that makes us Christians. When that is in place, we can't help but start living in a way that is more pleasing to Him. Through this relationship He is able to keep us aware of His will and purpose for us so that we can bear fruit in His name. **John 15:4**

Thank goodness God isn't looking for perfect because I am far from perfect in my relationship with Him, but I am seeking Him in many ways through His Word and prayer that I know will change my life. I pray each day that I can live in a way that pleases God and will inspire others to come to know Him intimately. That pastor at my church (Mike Lee) asked us a question a few weeks ago that I have thought about ever since. If you were arrested and convicted of being a Christ follower, would there be enough evidence to prove it? I pray for all of us that the judge would throw down his gavel and say, "Guilty!"

Relate – Can you relate to the message or theme? How? _____

_____

_____

_____

_____

_____

_____

Reread – Read the scriptures throughout today's message again.

_____

Revealed – Did God reveal anything new to you? Don't forget to come back and read them daily this week. God might not reveal to you today, but tomorrow.

_____

_____

_____

_____

_____

_____

Respond – Think about your week. Has God been whispering?

_____

_____

_____

_____

_____

_____

Reflect – Any other thoughts?

_____

_____

_____

_____

_____

_____

WEEK 12 ~ REALITY CHECK

Scriptures: 1 Corinthians 7:32-35, Psalm 13:2, Mark 4:19, Philippians 4:6-7

The start of school was just around the corner. Seriously, didn't they just get out!? I had dreaded my daughter starting kindergarten all summer. I thought the year would be easier, but I would miss having her at home. There is just something about sending her off to school for the day – out in the world where I can't watch over her, choose her playmates and be the one to give her a hug if she falls on the playground. Once you have children, you look at the world in a whole new way. It makes me feel very vulnerable. I have had to learn to trust God in a way I never did before. I know that He loves my children even more than I do, that He is the only one who can be with them EVERYWHERE they go and the only one who can truly protect them from the evil in this world.

When my children were young it was easy to fall into the trap of believing I could always protect them. They were small, couldn't walk, went to a church preschool for a few hours a day and were with me pretty much everywhere I went. Now that they are growing up, the reality of how much I AM NOT in control has really hit home. Each day, I have to pray for the courage and strength it takes to be a mom. Talk about trusting the Lord. I lean on Him in a way I could have never imagined before I had children.

There is an interesting scripture on marriage that I ran across in 1 Corinthians that puts scripture to my feelings. **I would like you to be free from concern. An unmarried man is concerned about the Lord's affairs – how he can please the Lord. But a married man is concerned about the affairs of this world – how he can please his wife – and his interests are divided. An unmarried woman or virgin is concerned about the Lord's affairs: Her aim is to be devoted to the Lord in both body and spirit. But a married woman is concerned about the affairs of this world – how she can please her husband. I am saying this for your own good, not to restrict you, but that you may live in a right way in undivided devotion to the Lord. 1 Corinthians 7:32-35**

Paul wasn't saying we shouldn't get married, but explaining how our emotions change when we have more than ourselves to think about. When we are married, have children or both, our interests are divided and we worry about the world's affairs because we want to protect the ones we love. We want to be around to love and protect them. Each day, I have to make the decision not to wrestle with thoughts that make my heart heavy with worry. I don't want the enemy to have control over me. **Psalm 13:2** I don't want the worries of this life to choke out all of the fruit God intends for me to produce. **Mark 4:19** Whether you worry about your children, marriage, job, safety or something else – present it before God. For it is only God who can grant us the peace, protection and understanding we all desire. **Philippians 4:6-7**

Relate – Can you relate to the message or theme? How? _____

_____

_____

_____

_____

_____

_____

Reread – Read the scriptures throughout today's message again.

_____

Revealed – Did God reveal anything new to you? Don't forget to come back and read them daily this week. God might not reveal to you today, but tomorrow.

_____

_____

_____

_____

_____

_____

Respond – Think about your week. Has God been whispering?

_____

_____

_____

_____

_____

_____

Reflect – Any other thoughts?

_____

_____

_____

_____

_____

_____

WEEK 13 ~ GOD SHOWS OFF

Scriptures: 1 Kings 18:24, Matthew 6:34

There are not many times in my life that I can say God has responded instantly to a prayer request I have laid before Him. This isn't to say that He hasn't answered my prayers – He has answered many of them. He just doesn't always do it instantly!

One summer night, I got one of those instant answers and it was amazing.

I was sitting on our bed doing my Bible study and felt the need to pray for God to show me His presence. We do have a God who adores us and wants more than anything to have a love relationship with us.

So I simply prayed, "Father, thank You for Your abiding love and guidance. I pray that You will show me Your presence and show off for me. Lord, blow my mind." Not even two minutes later the fire alarm in our whole apartment building went off! We had to wake up the kids and evacuate.

Talk about taking **1 Kings 18:24** to a new level.

Then you call on the name of your god, and I will call on the name of the LORD. The god who answers by fire – he is God. Then all the people said, "What you say is good."

Thank goodness He just answered by fire alarm and not a real fire, but He did answer! The fire alarm has even more significance for me personally. Since I was a little girl, I have always been afraid of my home catching on fire. I would pack all of my purses with my favorite toys and leave them by my window so I could toss them out and climb after them if our house caught on fire.

I think building our new home brought all of those worries about "fire" to the surface. For several weeks prior to my "instant" answer to prayer, I had been struggling with the worry of fire. I was giving it to God daily for Him to handle so that my mind would not become consumed with fear.

I have found that the only answer – the only formula – to get rid of fear in my life is to give it over to my Lord and Savior. Sometimes I can turn it over once and never worry again, but some things are a daily battle!

Therefore do not worry about tomorrow, for tomorrow will worry about itself. Each day has enough trouble of its own. Matthew 6:34

Relate – Can you relate to the message or theme? How? _____

_____
_____
_____
_____
_____
_____

Reread – Read the scriptures throughout today's message again.

_____

Revealed – Did God reveal anything new to you? Don't forget to come back and read them daily this week. God might not reveal to you today, but tomorrow.

_____
_____
_____
_____
_____
_____

Respond – Think about your week. Has God been whispering?

_____
_____
_____
_____
_____
_____

Reflect – Any other thoughts?

_____
_____
_____
_____
_____
_____

WEEK 14 ~ SEEK GOD FIRST

Scriptures: Psalm 14:2, Acts 17:26-27, Psalm 63:1

The LORD looks down from heaven on the sons of men to see if there are any who understand, any who seek God. Psalm 14:2

We are all guilty of this. We take our problems, our concerns and complaints to others before we take them to God. He is the one we should go to first when we are seeking wise counsel. God drove this point home to me over a year ago. It had been a tough few months. Everything seemed to be falling apart. My friend Shannon's cancer had spread to her brain, my Dad was diagnosed with prostate cancer, I had a disappointing birthday and oh, the list went on and on, but I will spare you. It was summer and all my friends were traveling, busy with camp, the pool, etc. When I tried to talk to them everyone seemed distracted. They were out of town or running out the door to the next activity or obligation. Don't get me wrong, I am guilty of the same thing. We get in a hurry and fill our schedules to the brim so there is no margin for the things that pop up.

After the fourth attempt to talk to a friend and getting nowhere . . . it hit me! God spoke to my heart and I realized I needed to be taking all of this worry and concern to God and trusting Him to be in control. Let me be clear, I'm not saying we don't need to seek the counsel of our friends. God has placed them in our lives to support us, love on us, give us solid Christian advice and hold us accountable. I praise God for my girlfriends everyday!

But the Bible says, From one man he made every nation of men, that they should inhabit the whole earth; and he determined the times set for them and the exact places where they should live. God did this so that men would seek him and perhaps reach out for him and find him, though he is not far from each one of us. Acts 17:26-27

I think God was reminding me that above all else, I should first seek Him. He is always available and "not far from each one of us." He is never on the way out the door, swim-team practice, Target or the grocery store. We have a God who craves a relationship with us and desires for us to seek Him daily. Next time you are troubled, have a concern or problem, talk it over with our Lord and Savior first. Seek His counsel, His comfort and direction. Pray that He provides you with a solution or answer in any way He can. He may speak straight to your heart, send a friend or put you in a circumstance that will give you the answer or peace that you need. He doesn't promise when or how, but He blesses all those who seek Him.

O God, you are my God, earnestly I seek you; my soul thirsts for you, my body longs for you, in a dry and weary land where there is no water. Psalm 63:1

Relate – Can you relate to the message or theme? How? _____

_____

_____

_____

_____

_____

_____

Reread – Read the scriptures throughout today's message again.

_____

Revealed – Did God reveal anything new to you? Don't forget to come back and read them daily this week. God might not reveal to you today, but tomorrow.

_____

_____

_____

_____

_____

_____

Respond – Think about your week. Has God been whispering?

_____

_____

_____

_____

_____

_____

Reflect – Any other thoughts?

_____

_____

_____

_____

_____

_____

WEEK 15 ~ LISTEN & OBEY

Scriptures: Deuteronomy 5:27, Hebrews 11, Hebrews 12:1-3

"Are you listening? Did you hear what I said? When I ask you to do something, you need to do it!" Oh, if I only had a penny for every time I have told my children to listen and obey.

Just this morning, I was reminding my children of how important it is for them to follow directions and do what I ask of them. Mid-sentence, I realized that this is what our Heavenly Father says to us each day as He speaks to us and we make the decision to listen and obey or move on with our own plan.

Go near and listen to all that the Lord our God says. Then tell us whatever the Lord our God tells you. We will listen and obey. Deuteronomy 5:27

When God nudges us we should obey immediately, but that sometimes takes a God-sized amount of faith. Do we have that much faith in our God? As Christians we can't just say that we have faith in God and His plan — we have to change our lives to reflect that we have faith in Him. If we don't step out and live like our God can do anything, why would others care to learn more about our God? When we step out on faith after God's nudging, and something happens that only God could do, people take notice. When we follow God's plan and not our own, He is able to do miraculous things that bless us and those around us. Many good things come from God's plan.

Hebrews 11 talks about faith and those in the Bible who demonstrated God-sized faith. This faith resulted in amazing and wonderful accomplishments – kingdoms were conquered, sinners turned to Christ, justice prevailed and many escaped death. But faith also resulted in some terrible scenarios as it was used to torture, imprison, put to death, mistreat and persecute. The outcomes of faith are not always pretty!

I know we all have the faith we need to follow God if we experience the good outcomes. The tough question is whether or not we have the faith to follow God when we endure the bad outcomes. I can say with confidence that our Father in Heaven has great rewards for those with faith; far more than this world could ever offer. Therefore, since we are surrounded by such a great cloud of witnesses, let us throw off everything that hinders and the sin that so easily entangles, and let us run with perseverance the race marked out for us. Let us fix our eyes on Jesus, the author and perfecter of our faith, who for the joy set before him endured the cross, scorning its shame, and sat down at the right hand of the throne of God. Consider Him who endured such opposition from sinful men, so that you will not grow weary and lose heart. **Hebrews 12:1-3**

Relate – Can you relate to the message or theme? How? _____

_____

_____

_____

_____

_____

Reread – Read the scriptures throughout today's message again.

_____

Revealed – Did God reveal anything new to you? Don't forget to come back and read them daily this week. God might not reveal to you today, but tomorrow.

_____

_____

_____

_____

_____

_____

Respond – Think about your week. Has God been whispering?

_____

_____

_____

_____

_____

Reflect – Any other thoughts?

_____

_____

_____

_____

_____

WEEK 16 ~ VICTORY

Scriptures: Proverbs 19:21, 1 Samuel 17, Joshua 6, Judges 7, 2 Chronicles 20:17

As soon as we pulled into the grocery store parking lot my son started plead-ing: "Can we PLEEEASE ride in the car cart mommy? Please?!" He loves driv-ing the car while I push the cart. "I'm not sure," I said. "Those carts are so big and heavy to push around." He continued, "But Mommy I sent you an e-mail about it."

I often try to tell God what I want to happen – how I want to do things and try to make Him change His plan to match mine. "But Father, I sent you an e-mail about this change in plans." Taking time to be still and know He is God is important so we are on track with His plan for us.

Many are the plans in a man's heart, but it is the Lord's purpose that prevails. Proverbs 19:21

God's purpose will prevail. The question is, do we want to jump in with faith and be a part of it? Or do we want to sit on the sidelines because it wasn't how we thought it was going to be? If we have been taking the time to sit with God and develop that personal relationship with Him, it's much easier to trust, have faith and take action. God doesn't want an e-mail. He wants a conversation. He wants your trust and your confidence.

There comes a point when we have to choose to believe God is who He says He is and can do all things. There are many great stories in the Bible of those who trusted God, followed His plan and found victory. Look at David when he faced Goliath, **1 Samuel 17** Joshua who walked around Jericho waiting for the walls to fall, **Joshua 6** Gideon as he sent most all of his army home before the battle, **Judges 7** all of the disciples as they left their professions and families to follow Christ.

Unbelief is costly, but there is *victory* when we choose to throw away our plan and human wisdom and put our faith in God's power and His plan!

You will not have to fight this battle. Take up your positions; stand firm and see the deliverance the LORD will give you, O Judah and Jerusalem. Do not be afraid; do not be discouraged. Go out to face them tomorrow, and the LORD will be with you. 2 Chronicles 20:17

Relate – Can you relate to the message or theme? How? _____

_____

_____

_____

_____

_____

_____

Reread – Read the scriptures throughout today's message again.

_____

Revealed – Did God reveal anything new to you? Don't forget to come back and read them daily this week. God might not reveal to you today, but tomorrow.

_____

_____

_____

_____

_____

_____

Respond – Think about your week. Has God been whispering?

_____

_____

_____

_____

_____

_____

Reflect – Any other thoughts?

_____

_____

_____

_____

_____

_____

WEEK 17 ~ WAIT

Scriptures: Isaiah 40:31, Psalm 73:26

Why is it so difficult to wait on the Lord to answer our prayers or direct us to serve His purpose? There are so many scriptures that tell us how important it is to "wait" on the Lord. One of my favorites is:

They that *wait* upon the Lord shall renew their *strength*; they shall mount up with wings as eagles; they shall run, and not be weary; and they shall walk, and not faint. Isaiah 40:31

I know that if I am waiting on anything, I feel like I am wasting time or I am being inefficient. Inefficiency is a pet peeve of mine, so it can be tough on me. However, I have discovered that waiting for God to speak is neither inefficient nor inactive. It is a time to dig deeper, pray more and develop a more intimate relationship with Him. It is not up to us to figure out the answers – all the responsibility is God's. We are trying to accomplish His outcome, not ours. Really, doesn't that just take a load off your shoulders? We don't have to figure it out. We just have to wait and respond in obedience. I am so thankful I don't have to come up with the plan. I just need to do the work.

Think about how often we say, "Oh, to be a kid again. No worries, just fun! Someone makes all the decisions and takes care of everything for you." That's us! We are still kids in our Father's eyes. We don't have to figure it all out on our own. More than anything, He wants us to be still, know Him, understand Him and wait for His whisper. Like our own kids, who want everything RIGHT NOW, we are the same. But I am trying to put the frustration and impatience aside and treasure the waiting. I'm trying to appreciate the fact that "waiting" is taking me closer to God and taking me into a deeper relationship with Him. There is always a lesson in the waiting and it might just be that until we learn that lesson our Father can't give us the answer we are longing for.

While I wait for answers, direction, understanding and clarification, our Lord is the **strength of my heart. Psalm 73:26** I couldn't face the day without His strength!

My flesh and my heart may fail, but God is the *strength of my heart* and my portion forever. Psalm 73:26

Relate – Can you relate to the message or theme? How? _____

_____

_____

_____

_____

_____

Reread – Read the scriptures throughout today's message again.

_____

Revealed – Did God reveal anything new to you? Don't forget to come back and read them daily this week. God might not reveal to you today, but tomorrow.

_____

_____

_____

_____

_____

_____

Respond – Think about your week. Has God been whispering?

_____

_____

_____

_____

_____

_____

Reflect – Any other thoughts?

_____

_____

_____

_____

_____

_____

WEEK 18 ~ THE CONSTANT BATTLE

Scriptures: Ephesians 4:27, Hebrews 6:19, Psalm 43:3, Jude 1:24, Jude 1:9

"God wants us to beat up all the bad guys!" my son stated with conviction. He was trying to convince my daughter of something she knew to be false, but he said it so boldly she stopped mid-conversation and had me confirm that his statement was false. I thought this was such a great illustration of how Satan works in our lives. We know our God! We know His promises! He never changes. He forgives. He loves. He is faithful and honest. The list of His wondrous qualities goes on and on. However, when Satan starts to bend our ear we begin to question what we know of God and ourselves.

Satan can be so convincing that the things we are certain of one day – we distrust the next. We have to know our Heavenly Father inside and out, we need to trust Him and find comfort in His promises. When we know God intimately, we will be able to discern the truth and see through Satan's schemes. As soon as Satan anticipates a weakness or lack of faith on our end, he will begin to attack. **And do not give the devil a foothold. Ephesians 4:27** We have to stand firm. God is our hope and **we have this hope as an anchor for the soul, firm and secure. Hebrews 6:19**

I do believe Satan is real. I do believe his lies, deceptions and sins swirl around us every day. It is war, but I choose not to focus on him. Our Savior sealed his fate. He is defeated! Our Father in Heaven should be our focus and our guide. The only way Satan can affect us is if we choose to believe him over God.

Send forth your light and your truth, let them guide me; let them bring me to your holy mountain, to the place where you dwell. Psalm 43:3

Choose to look straight ahead, fix your gaze directly before you. Psalm 4:25 For before you, is our Father in Heaven who only has plans to prosper us and give us a hope and a future. Jeremiah 29:11 He is able. He can do all things. He will give you rest. He will never leave you. These things are true. They are not deceptions! If you have been the victim of worry, anxiety, depression, guilt, resentment or anger. . . change your focus. Turn your back on Satan, his lies and betrayal. **Look to the only one who is able to keep you from falling and to present you before His glorious presence without fault and with great joy. Jude 1:24** Trust God and He will handle the rest. **But even the archangel Michael, when he was disputing with the devil about the body of Moses, did not dare to bring a slanderous accusation against him, but said, "The Lord rebuke you!" Jude 1:9**

Relate – Can you relate to the message or theme? How? _____

_____
_____
_____
_____
_____
_____

Reread – Read the scriptures throughout today's message again.

_____

Revealed – Did God reveal anything new to you? Don't forget to come back and read them daily this week. God might not reveal to you today, but tomorrow.

_____
_____
_____
_____
_____
_____

Respond – Think about your week. Has God been whispering?

_____
_____
_____
_____
_____
_____

Reflect – Any other thoughts?

_____
_____
_____
_____
_____
_____

WEEK 19 ~ EAT WHAT YOU CRAVE!?

Scriptures: Romans 8:5, Romans 13:14, Romans 8:8, Psalm 25:15

"Eat What You Crave." This was an actual advertisement on a billboard we passed while taking a family road trip. I was shocked when I saw it, but found it thought-provoking.

These four words summed it all up for me. This is exactly the kind of world we live in. Our minds are filled with constant messages from the media, advertisements and Internet that if it feels good, we should go for it. We are bombarded with the idea that if it feels good, do it – eat it, if you want it badly enough – do whatever it takes.

In this self-absorbed world, there are more than enough pits to fall in, sins to overcome and temptations to resist. They are around every corner and in almost every situation we face. We must stay grounded in Christ, focused on His Word and, as Beth Moore says, "Live life one surrendered day at a time. Eyes to the East, hands to the cross, feet to the path." **Clothe yourself with the Lord Jesus Christ, and do not think about how to gratify the desires of the sinful nature. Romans 13:14**

We were all born sinners, but we don't have to give into sin. When we are controlled by sinful nature we can't please God. **Romans 8:8** We need to choose God over sin. I once read that when the "Lord Jesus is in the center of your life He takes care of the circumference as well." With Christ in the center of our lives, our thoughts and hearts can overcome our sinful nature.

Those who live according to the sinful nature have their minds set on what that nature desires; but those who live in accordance with the Spirit have their minds set on what the Spirit desires. Romans 8:5

I am not saying this is easy. Let's face it , we wouldn't be so drawn to sin if it wasn't fun. Just think about the '60s. God doesn't give us rules, laws and commandments because He wants to control us. He knows how hurtful the results of sin can be to us and others. He wants to protect us from harm the same way we want to protect our own children. Choose to conquer your sinful nature! *Eyes on the Lord!*

My eyes are ever on the LORD, for only he will release my feet from the snare. Psalm 25:15

Relate – Can you relate to the message or theme? How? _____

_____
_____
_____
_____
_____
_____

Reread – Read the scriptures throughout today's message again.

_____

Revealed – Did God reveal anything new to you? Don't forget to come back and read them daily this week. God might not reveal to you today, but tomorrow.

_____
_____
_____
_____
_____
_____

Respond – Think about your week. Has God been whispering?

_____
_____
_____
_____
_____
_____

Reflect – Any other thoughts?

_____
_____
_____
_____
_____
_____

WEEK 20 ~ THE DESERT PLACE

Scriptures: Exodus 7:16, 3:18, 5:1, 16:10, Psalm 78:15, 78:52, 136:16

A friend recently asked me to pray for her. She expressed how she was in a "dry" place and didn't know of anything specific that I could pray, but she just felt she needed a lift. Her request made me think back on times in my own life when I felt like I was in the desert or a dry place with the Lord. Webster's Online Dictionary defines desert as: 1) arid land with usually sparse vegetation; an area of water apparently devoid of life 2) a wild uninhabited and uncultivated tract 3) a desolate or forbidding area.

That definition certainly doesn't make you want to book an airline ticket and head off to the desert for your next vacation. As Christians, these "desert times" can be stressful, scary and can make us question our relationship with God and question God Himself. I want to look at the desert in a different light and give it a new definition. If you search for scriptures throughout the book of Exodus, you notice that God called His people to: worship me in the desert, **Exodus 7:16** journey into the desert to offer sacrifices to the Lord our God, **Exodus 3:18** hold a festival to me in the desert. **Exodus 5:1** They looked toward the desert, and there was the glory of the LORD appearing in the cloud. **Exodus 16:10**

My point is that the desert can be a good place, but it is up to us to meet God there with an open mind and a trusting heart. If God is there with us – and we believe that He is who He says He is – we can praise Him in that desert place. On the flip side, the desert can be all that Webster's describes if we lose sight of God and start to grumble as the Israelites did on their well-known journey through the desert. A trip through the desert with God can provide festival, praise, growth and worship, or a trip through the desert without Him can bring thirst, defeat and death.

We know God speaks to us in four main ways: prayer, the Bible, the church and our circumstances. Let's not forget the last one. Our circumstances can bring us to that desert place and, if we open our heart to the Lord, He can fill it with answers and speak to us in ways we wouldn't hear or understand if we were not in the desert. I believe during the "dry times" we learn to seek God daily, ask Him questions, get to know Him more intimately and remember not to take Him for granted. It can be a great example of how much we need Him in our daily lives, how much He has to offer and how much we count on Him.

So, let's redefine desert as: 1) vast land that grows the bread of life; an area filled with the living water 2) a wild and exciting area full of opportunities to gain knowledge and grow closer with our Father in Heaven 3) an intimate and pleasant area. Now that's better!

He split the rocks in the desert and gave them water as abundant as the seas; Psalm 78:15 But he brought his people out like a flock; he led them like sheep through the desert. Psalm 78:52 To him who led his people through the desert, His love endures forever. Psalm 136:16

Relate – Can you relate to the message or theme? How? _____

_____

_____

_____

_____

_____

_____

Reread – Read the scriptures throughout today's message again.

_____

Revealed – Did God reveal anything new to you? Don't forget to come back and read them daily this week. God might not reveal to you today, but tomorrow.

_____

_____

_____

_____

_____

_____

Respond – Think about your week. Has God been whispering?

_____

_____

_____

_____

_____

_____

Reflect – Any other thoughts?

_____

_____

_____

_____

_____

_____

WEEK 21 ~ LIFT UP YOUR HANDS

Scriptures: Psalm 70:4, 2 Samuel 6:14-15

I recently saw a picture of a friend at an NC State basketball game. He was up in the stands with both arms raised, making the wolf sign with his fingers, wearing his NC State red and passionately cheering mouth-wide-open for his team.

It struck me like a ton of bricks. So many people attend rock concerts and sports games, raise their hands, cheer and worship the team, singers or players. Why can't people walk into church and feel like they can do the same thing?! It is certainly a prime example of how our society elevates music, sports, self and Hollywood above all else, and sometimes we get sucked in. It is OK to join the crowds at sporting events or concerts in wild praise, but how about in church?

I am not going to tell you that I have always been comfortable worshipping with such emotion: hands in the air, eyes closed and soaking in the comforting and inspiring words of the music. However, as my relationship with God has grown more intimate, I am unable to keep from responding to His glory and majesty in a physical way.

But may all who seek you
rejoice and be glad in you;
may those who love your salvation always say,
"Let God be exalted!" Psalm 70:4

Church and worship feel incomplete if I haven't had an opportunity to sing, praise and worship my Father in Heaven. I love to read **2 Samuel 6:14-15** and imagine David singing and dancing with great abandon before GOD.

David, wearing a linen ephod, danced before the LORD with all his might, while he and the entire house of Israel brought up the ark of the LORD with shouts and the sound of trumpets.

Have you danced with great abandon before God recently? Have you let your hair down and shown Him with praise how much He means to you and how thankful you are for His many blessings?

42

Relate – Can you relate to the message or theme? How? _____

_____

_____

_____

_____

_____

Reread – Read the scriptures throughout today's message again.

_____

Revealed – Did God reveal anything new to you? Don't forget to come back and read them daily this week. God might not reveal to you today, but tomorrow.

_____

_____

_____

_____

_____

Respond – Think about your week. Has God been whispering?

_____

_____

_____

_____

_____

Reflect – Any other thoughts?

_____

_____

_____

_____

_____

WEEK 22 ~ GODCHICK

Scriptures: Job 13:9, Luke 12:48, Romans 14:12, Deuteronomy 11:26-28

A few years ago my husband gave me a bracelet for my birthday. It was silver with "GODCHICK" engraved on it. I loved it, but eventually the bracelet wore out and I decided to make it the personalized license plate on my car. I'll tell you, that can put a lot of pressure on a person when you're driving around town and everyone knows you're a Christian. No cutting people off or losing your temper. You get the picture! I have even thought to myself, "Maybe I should take it off." It is a lot of responsibility, and what if I can't live up to the example I need to set as GOD-CHICK? What if I need to scream at my kids one morning on the way to school because they won't stop arguing? Then I reconsidered and took a tough look at myself. Why does it take a license plate to make me feel accountable? It should be that I want to please God and live in such a way that brings others closer to Him. Hypocrite! That is what so many Christians are accused of and why so many others turn away from Christianity. We talk one way but live another. I don't want that to be me. How about you? Even if we can fool others, we can never fool God. **Job 13:9**

But the one who does not know and does things deserving punishment will be beaten with few blows. From everyone who has been given much, much will be demanded; and from the one who has been entrusted with much, much more will be asked. Luke 12:48

No one said it would be easy. As this scripture states, those who receive much are held to great accountability. As Christians, we receive the greatest gift that can be given – complete forgiveness, atonement for all sins and eternal life with our Father in Heaven. If that doesn't inspire us to live our lives as an example of His love, I don't think there is anything else that could, not even a license plate!

We will be held accountable for all we do and say in this life. We will all give an account to God. **Romans 14:12** We need to take God's Word and our responsibilities as Christians very seriously. Do this out of a love for our Lord and Savior, not just for looks or reputation. As an exercise, for the next week imagine a big sign hanging around your neck that says, "I am a Christian!" Or if you are really brave, wear a shirt that says it! See how your words and actions change.

See, I am setting before you today a blessing and a curse – the blessing if you obey the commands of the LORD your God that I am giving you today; the curse if you disobey the commands of the LORD your God and turn from the way that I command you today by following other gods, which you have not known. Deuteronomy 11:26-28

Relate – Can you relate to the message or theme? How? _____

_____

_____

_____

_____

_____

_____

Reread – Read the scriptures throughout today's message again.

_____

Revealed – Did God reveal anything new to you? Don't forget to come back and read them daily this week. God might not reveal to you today, but tomorrow.

_____

_____

_____

_____

_____

_____

Respond – Think about your week. Has God been whispering?

_____

_____

_____

_____

_____

_____

Reflect – Any other thoughts?

_____

_____

_____

_____

_____

_____

WEEK 23 ~ UNCONDITIONAL LOVE

Scriptures: Joel 2:13, Psalm 36:7, Isaiah 54:10, 44:22, 43:25

My son came into the kitchen crying. He was upset with his sister. Apparently, *he* had hit her and she was mad at him for that. If you are a mom, I am sure you have heard it all before! So, we had a talk about hitting, why it wasn't kind, why people don't like it, you get the drift. Then he said to me, "Mommy, why do you always love me?"

My first response was a thought, "I am so thankful he understands that even though I don't love his actions, I always love him." My second response was an answer to his question and honestly, it felt very weak as I looked at him and said, "I always love you because I am your mom and you are my son." Seriously, couldn't I come up with anything more creative and inspiring than that? Thankfully, it was good enough for him, and off he went.

Isn't that how it is with us and God? We are his children, and when we have sinned or done something terrible we sit at his feet and say, "How can you still love me? How can you possibly forgive this?" **Return to the LORD your God, for he is gracious and compassionate, slow to anger and abounding in love, and he relents from sending calamity. Joel 2:13**

His answer is so simple, it doesn't seem like enough. It feels like we should have to do more, pay a bigger price or suffer some sort of punishment. No! He forgives because He is our Father and His love for us is deep, constant and unconditional. **"Though the mountains be shaken and the hills be removed, yet my unfailing love for you will not be shaken nor my covenant of peace be removed," says the LORD, who has compassion on you." Isaiah 54:10** If that love didn't exist, if he didn't love us as He says He does, there is no way He could have allowed His son to die on that cross for us.

God forgiving us – that is the easy part. The question usually is, can we accept that forgiveness and move forward? **I, even I, am he who blots out your transgressions, for my own sake, and remembers your sins no more. Isaiah 43:25**

Trust Him. Believe in Him. Follow Him. Celebrate Him. You are forgiven. God washes our sins away daily and allows us the opportunity to start each day with a fresh start. Take advantage of it. Rejoice in it. Don't allow the bondage of sin to hold you down, harden your heart, make you lose your way or lead you into more temptation. God's love is priceless; take refuge in the shadow of His wings. **Psalm 36:7**

I have swept away your offenses like a cloud, your sins like the morning mist. Return to me, for I have redeemed you. Isaiah 44:22

Relate – Can you relate to the message or theme? How? _____

_____

_____

_____

_____

_____

_____

Reread – Read the scriptures throughout today's message again.

_____

Revealed – Did God reveal anything new to you? Don't forget to come back and read them daily this week. God might not reveal to you today, but tomorrow.

_____

_____

_____

_____

_____

_____

Respond – Think about your week. Has God been whispering?

_____

_____

_____

_____

_____

_____

Reflect – Any other thoughts?

_____

_____

_____

_____

_____

_____

WEEK 24 ~ IS GOD ON YOUR SHELF?

Scriptures: Matthew 1:23, Colossians 2:13, Psalm 51:10, Galatians 3:26-28, Jeremiah 29:11

Christmas was around the corner, and our "Elf on the Shelf" returned to keep watch over the kids. He reports back to Santa every night with the details of who has been naughty and nice. I don't have a ton of trouble with my kids, but there is something about that elf. He is a huge motivator around the holidays. My children remind each other daily: Be careful what you say, you better not hit, you better say "please." All because the elf is watching and they are trying to earn the delivery of toys that may be coming on Jesus' birthday.

What if we lived our lives like this? If we would realize and understand that God is always with us, knows all we do, all we think and all we plan before we even do it? Can you imagine how we would change the way we do things?

The virgin will be with child and will give birth to a son, and they will call him Immanuel, which means, God with us. Matthew 1:23

We don't need to be good and obey God's commandments because we want the BIG prize – salvation, love, grace. He has already given us that. We aren't worthy, but He has given it to us anyway. It is ours if we just accept it – if we just accept Him. **When you were dead in your sins and in the uncircumcision of your sinful nature, God made you alive with Christ. He forgave us all our sins. Colossians 2:13**

God doesn't force us to live according to His Word. We live according to His Word and commandments because we choose to. We choose to honor Him, we choose to show others His kindness and grace, and we choose to forgive the unforgivable. No, it is not easy and we are not capable if we try to do it alone, but with Christ we CAN! **Create in me a pure heart, O God, and renew a steadfast spirit within me. Psalm 51:10**

If we clothe ourselves in Christ, **Galatians 3:26-28** soak in His Word, listen for His whisper and trust Him for all our provisions, our actions will come naturally. His kindness, love, compassion, forgiveness and grace will flow out of us and spill onto everyone we come in contact with. We don't have a God on the shelf who is watching to see if we deserve His love! We have an active, living God who loves us, who wants to know us intimately, help us navigate our lives in the best way possible and use us as instruments of His peace and love.

"For I know the plans I have for you," declares the LORD, "plans to prosper you and not to harm you, plans to give you hope and a future." Jeremiah 29:11

Relate – Can you relate to the message or theme? How? _____

_____

_____

_____

_____

_____

_____

Reread – Read the scriptures throughout today's message again.

_____

Revealed – Did God reveal anything new to you? Don't forget to come back and read them daily this week. God might not reveal to you today, but tomorrow.

_____

_____

_____

_____

_____

_____

Respond – Think about your week. Has God been whispering?

_____

_____

_____

_____

_____

_____

Reflect – Any other thoughts?

_____

_____

_____

_____

_____

_____

WEEK 25 ~ HAVING ISSUES?

Scriptures: 2 Timothy 3:16, Proverbs 3:5, Proverbs16:9, Psalm 32:8, 37:7

As I have mentioned in previous devotions, God frequently uses my children to teach me valuable lessons. Their adorable and sometimes profound statements can stop me in my tracks and make me consider a deeper message. On the way to preschool one morning my son said, "Mommy, I need to go to the doctor. I need some issues medicine because I am having issues!" Oh, I got a wonderful laugh from his adorable statement, and I replied, "You know what? We all have issues and some 'issues' medication would be great. I wish they made that."

Oh course, as my wheels started turning and I thought more about what he said, I heard the whisper: "It does exist. There has always been a medication for any issue you have. It is the Bible, God's written Word." Why isn't the Bible the *first* place we turn when we are faced with a problem or issue? If we are sick we go to the doctor, if we need advice we call a friend, if we have a legal issue we call a lawyer . . . the list goes on and on. What if our first stop was God and His Word? I wonder how many issues could be resolved by just stopping and having some quiet time with the Lord? **All Scripture is God-breathed and is useful for teaching, rebuking, correcting and training in righteousness. 2 Timothy 3:16**

Everything we need to know in order to live our lives to the fullest is in the Bible. God has provided the answers and direction. All we have to do is open the book, our hearts and soak it in. If our car is broken we go the mechanic because we know he has the skills to fix the problem. Usually, we don't even know the mechanic and we still trust him to fix our car. As Christians, we say we know our God. We say we trust Him and that we love Him. Let's live that example, not just say it. Let's trust our God to come through for us. Let's be patient while we wait for His plan or for Him to help us tackle our "issue(s)." **Trust in the Lord with all your heart, and lean not on your own understanding; in all your ways acknowledge Him, and He shall direct your paths. Proverbs 3:5** When I approach God in prayer to discern His will in a situation, I simply say, "Father, I don't want to do this if it isn't Your will because if I do it and it isn't in Your plan it won't work and will just be a big mess. So please guide me and lead me in Your direction, not my own." **A man's heart plans his way, but the Lord directs his steps. Proverbs 16:9**

Now, I would love to tell you that I approach every situation like this and that I take everything to God first, but I can't. However, I am trying to become more obedient and take this approach with every detail of my life. I have learned (the hard way) that I am incapable of doing anything without the Lord by my side. Alone, my skills are completely inadequate! I couldn't face a day as a mom, wife, daughter, friend, volunteer or sister without knowing that my Lord is **instructing me and teaching me in the way I should go and guiding me with His eye. Psalm 32:8.** What a peace that can bring if we only accept it. Rest in the Lord, and wait patiently for Him. **Psalm 37:7**

Relate – Can you relate to the message or theme? How? _____

_____

_____

_____

_____

_____

_____

Reread – Read the scriptures throughout today's message again.

_____

Revealed – Did God reveal anything new to you? Don't forget to come back and read them daily this week. God might not reveal to you today, but tomorrow.

_____

_____

_____

_____

_____

_____

Respond – Think about your week. Has God been whispering?

_____

_____

_____

_____

_____

_____

Reflect – Any other thoughts?

_____

_____

_____

_____

_____

_____

WEEK 26 ~ LOVE VS. FEAR

Scriptures: Jeremiah 29:11, Jeremiah 31:3, Zephaniah 3:17, John15:3, 15:9,
Ephesians 3:16-21

I have been reading my son *Star Wars: The Clone War* books. He loves them and I confess I do too. I even enjoyed *Star Wars* as a child. Yoda is one of my favorite characters. "Yoda (the great *Star Wars* Jedi) said that fear is a way to the dark side of the Force." Even the little green guy gets it. Fear can destroy us, our faith, our trust and our focus on what is good and right. Fear can certainly lead us to the "dark side." Only, in our lives, the dark side is sin and Satan – not Darth Vader. One of the things I fear the most is something happening to one of my children. I have learned to recognize it before it paralyzes me. In fact, as soon as I begin to take on that worry and fear creeps in, I give it to God. I wish I could say I never faltered and I never tried to take back the steering wheel, but I can't. The truth is I have to hand over my fears to God almost daily. I have to trust in Him and His love for me and my family. My children are, after all, His children before they are mine. God has entrusted them to me, but they are just on loan from Him. As a mom, it is difficult to imagine, but I know that He loves them more than I do. The word love (loves, loved) is mentioned almost 700 times in the NIV.

"For I know the plans I have for you," declares the LORD, "plans to prosper you and not to harm you, plans to give you hope and a future." Jeremiah 29:11 The LORD appeared to us in the past, saying: "I have loved you with an everlasting love; I have drawn you with loving-kindness" Jeremiah 31:3 The LORD your God is with you, he is mighty to save. He will take great delight in you, he will quiet you with his love, he will rejoice over you with singing." Zephaniah 3:17 Greater love has no one than this, that he lay down his life for his friends. John 15:13 As the Father has loved me, so have I loved you. Now remain in my love. John 15:9

These are just a few scriptures that describe the awesome love that our God has for each one of us. Have you ever tried to write a love letter or note to someone and express how much he or she means to you? Even for the best writer, it can be difficult to find words that express those deep emotions. For many, words aren't enough. We need to do something tangible for someone to express our love: visiting, mowing a yard, making a meal, sending a card, etc. Our God has done more than that for us. Not only did He leave us the descriptions and promises of His vast love for us in the Bible, He proved it when He allowed His son to die for us. Oh, He is all about LOVE. Love we can't even comprehend. The questions I am contemplating today are: How can we let fear control us when we have someone who loves us more than we can comprehend? How can we let fear control us when we have the ultimate protector? How can we let fear control us when we have someone who has laid down His life for us leading us on the path of life? What is your greatest fear? Do you trust that God is bigger than your fear(s)? Do you find comfort and rest in His infinite love? Let the one who loves you more than anyone else sit in the driver's seat of your life. You have nothing to fear from Him. Please read **Ephesians 3:16-21.**

Relate – Can you relate to the message or theme? How? _____

_____

_____

_____

_____

_____

_____

Reread – Read the scriptures throughout today's message again.

_____

Revealed – Did God reveal anything new to you? Don't forget to come back and read them daily this week. God might not reveal to you today, but tomorrow.

_____

_____

_____

_____

_____

_____

Respond – Think about your week. Has God been whispering?

_____

_____

_____

_____

_____

_____

Reflect – Any other thoughts?

_____

_____

_____

_____

_____

_____

WEEK 27 ~ EMPTY

Scriptures: Proverbs 4:23, Philippians 4:7, Psalm 26:2

When my daughter was 3 1/2, she had to have another set of tubes put in her ears. We were at the doctor's office getting all of her pre-op papers in order. While we were waiting, she picked up a stethoscope, put the eartips in her ears and placed the chestpiece on her heart. She looked up at me with a smile and said, "Mommy, I hear God in my heart!"

Wouldn't it be nice if that was all we had to do to hear God working in our hearts? Especially the times when God seems to be silent and our hearts feel empty. In the past, I have written about the struggles and benefits of our hearts being in that "desert" place, but I think this is different. I think we can be close to God, but our hearts can feel empty because of a circumstance we are dealing with, an answer we are waiting on from the Lord, a lesson we are learning, a broken promise, deception from someone we have trusted, etc.

Above all else, guard your heart, for it is the wellspring of life. Proverbs 4:23

As I looked up Bible passages that referenced the heart, I read that the heart can harden, weep, rejoice, yearn, fail, soften, grieve, hate, fear, praise, desire, despise, instruct, fight, love, discern, change, commit, seek and the list goes on. Every emotion we feel comes from the heart. The heart can lead us down the right path if we guard it from emotions that eat away at its core and leave us feeling empty.

And the peace of God, which transcends all understanding, will guard your hearts and your minds in Christ Jesus. Philippians 4:7

Our prayer must be for God to fill our hearts with His love, praise, joy, peace, instruction, gladness and forgiveness. If we fill our hearts with all of these righteous things and pray for God's protection, how could there be room for the things that leave us empty? However, I guarantee that if there is one spot in your heart that is not filled up by the Lord, Satan will find his way in with greed, anger, fear, guilt . . . whatever will fit.

Test me, O LORD, and try me, examine my heart and my mind; Psalm 26:2

Put on your stethoscope today and listen to your heart. Pray for God to reveal the weaknesses in your heart so that you can confront them, resolve them and clean them out.

Relate – Can you relate to the message or theme? How? _____

_____

_____

_____

_____

_____

_____

Reread – Read the scriptures throughout today's message again.

_____

Revealed – Did God reveal anything new to you? Don't forget to come back and read them daily this week. God might not reveal to you today, but tomorrow.

_____

_____

_____

_____

_____

_____

Respond – Think about your week. Has God been whispering?

_____

_____

_____

_____

_____

_____

Reflect – Any other thoughts?

_____

_____

_____

_____

_____

_____

WEEK 28 ~ MASKS

Scriptures: Psalm 25:20, Ephesians 6:13. 1:22 & 3:7

Masks! We have all worn them and most of us still do. Maybe not every day, maybe just around certain people or in certain circumstances. No, not the cute or scary masks we wear on Halloween or in a play. The masks we wear to cover up pain, shame, depression, fear or resentment that has taken up residence in our hearts.

For years, I wore a mask of shame and guilt about past decisions I had made. Decisions that had hurt others along the way. I had worn the mask so long I didn't remember how to take it off or even what I looked like underneath it. God was nudging me to share my story. I didn't want to do it, but I knew in my heart I had to. After sharing my story with a wonderful group of women in my Bible study, I was finally able to take off the mask. I didn't have to hide anymore. I found shelter under my Father's wing and in a caring group of friends who loved me regardless of my past. I felt His forgiveness pour over me and realized how silly and wasteful it had been for me to wait all those years to accept His forgiveness and shed the mask.

Guard my life and rescue me; let me not be put to shame, for I take refuge in you. Psalm 25:20

I don't think I had ever truly known God until that moment. I finally understood that being a Christian was more about a relationship than it was about a religion. This was a huge turning point in my life. After I threw away the mask I had been wearing all those years, I was able to put on the armor of God and He was able to start using me for His Glory and His ministry. Satan no longer had a grip on me. I believed and knew God could use me to accomplish His will. I praise Him for that. I can say we have an *awesome God* because I have experienced it personally. **Put on the full armor of God so that you can take your stand against the devil's schemes. Ephesians 6:13**

My prayer for each of you today is that if you are wearing a mask, you will find the courage to put it down at our Master's feet and leave it with Him. **And God placed all things under his feet and appointed him to be head over everything for the church. Ephesians 1:22** Accept the gift He has for you: peace, healing, restoration, forgiveness and love. Leave it with Him and go out with a grateful heart that is ready to serve the Lord with passion and praise. **I became a servant of this gospel by the gift of God's grace given me through the working of his power. Ephesians 3:7**

We can't truly be His servants in this world until we have allowed Him into our lives to heal our wounds and make us whole again. **Each one should use whatever gift he has received to serve others, faithfully administering God's grace in its various forms. 1 Peter 4:10**

Relate – Can you relate to the message or theme? How? _____

_____

_____

_____

_____

_____

Reread – Read the scriptures throughout today's message again.

_____

Revealed – Did God reveal anything new to you? Don't forget to come back and read them daily this week. God might not reveal to you today, but tomorrow.

_____

_____

_____

_____

_____

_____

Respond – Think about your week. Has God been whispering?

_____

_____

_____

_____

_____

_____

Reflect – Any other thoughts?

_____

_____

_____

_____

_____

_____

WEEK 29 ~ PLEASE PASS THE SALT

Scriptures: Colossians 4:5-6, James 3:8, 1:26, 3:5, 3:1, 1 Peter 3:9-11, Colossians 4:5-6

Now that my children are older, I have learned you can't say anything "off the radar." Somehow, those little ears always hear it. It is a lot of work to raise our children to be Christians in this self-centered world, but even more work for us to consistently model it for them! "Mommy, you know that little boy who always calls me a baby at school? Well, I saw him today and he stuck his tongue out at me. He *DOES NOT* have God in his heart." My child's comment diffused my irritation and reminded me of what the appropriate response should be. "Well, I guess we better add him to our prayer list tonight and pray that God finds His way into his heart." **Be wise in the way you act toward outsiders; make the most of every opportunity. Let your conversation be always full of grace, seasoned with salt, so that you may know how to answer everyone. Colossians 4:5-6**

I'll be honest, my tongue can my greatest enemy if I am not careful. I guess I need a little more salt in my diet! I have spent many days reading the book of James because he has a lot to say about taming the tongue. I have learned that **no man can tame the tongue. It is a restless evil, full of deadly poison. James 3:8** We have to rely on the strength and direction of our Lord to fill us with grace and His Word to season us so that our conversations and words are used to build up and not destroy. **If anyone considers himself religious and yet does not keep a tight rein on his tongue, he deceives himself and his religion is worthless. James 1:26**

James 1:26 changed my view on words and the tongue more than anything else. In The Message, this scripture reads, **Anyone who sets himself up as "religious" by talking a good game is self-deceived. This kind of religion is hot air and only hot air.** More than anything, I don't want this to be me. I don't want to be full of hot air! **[T]he tongue is a small part of the body, but it makes great boasts. Consider what a great forest is set on fire by a small spark. James 3:5.** I realize that I will bring judgment from others by putting my thoughts, feelings, lessons learned and encouragement out there in print. **Not many of you should presume to be teachers, my brothers, because you know that we who teach will be judged more strictly. James 3:1** You don't have to teach a Bible study, share the message of God with others, teach Sunday school, write a blog or volunteer at church to be judged. If you call yourself a Christian, you too will be judged more strictly. As true Christians we can't **repay evil with evil or insult with insult, but with blessing, because to this you were called so that you may inherit a blessing. For, Whoever would love life and see good days must keep his tongue from evil and his lips from deceitful speech. He must turn from evil and do good; he must seek peace and pursue it. 1 Peter 3:9-11** Words can hurt! We have all been the victim of an unruly or angry tongue. Like a forest fire that starts out with a small spark, hurtful words can fuel a fire within us that leads to more evil and insults. Our job is to turn the evil or insult into a blessing. The dictionary says salt (verb) is used "to cure, preserve, or treat with salt." Let our Father in Heaven season you, cure you, preserve you and treat you through His scriptures so that your tongue does not overcome you.

Relate – Can you relate to the message or theme? How? _____

_____

_____

_____

_____

_____

Reread – Read the scriptures throughout today's message again.

_____

Revealed – Did God reveal anything new to you? Don't forget to come back and read them daily this week. God might not reveal to you today, but tomorrow.

_____

_____

_____

_____

_____

Respond – Think about your week. Has God been whispering?

_____

_____

_____

_____

_____

Reflect – Any other thoughts?

_____

_____

_____

_____

_____

WEEK 30 ~ ALIENS AMONG US

Scriptures: 1 Peter 2:11, Hebrews 11:13-16, Ecclesiastes 3:11-12

"Cross your fingers!" he said. "Oh, I'll do more than that," I explained. "I'll pray about it." Silence and an awkward laugh led the way to the next topic.

Sometimes, I forget I am a foreigner in this world. A resident of another place, with only a temporary address on this planet. I get the "look" more often than not. All I have to do is drive up in GODCHICK, mention church, Bible study, prayer, etc. and there it is. It can be like telling someone you just got over the swine flu! They slowly back away.

In **1 Peter 2:11**, the Bible even calls us **aliens and strangers in this world**. God knew we would feel like this. He created us to long for Him. This is not our home. Our place is with Him. We will only find satisfaction and contentment when we are with our Father in Heaven.

All these people were still living by faith when they died. They did not receive the things promised; they only saw them and welcomed them from a distance. And they admitted that they were aliens and strangers on earth. People who say such things show that they are looking for a country of their own. If they had been thinking of the country they had left, they would have had opportunity to return. Instead, they were longing for a better country – a heavenly one. Therefore God is not ashamed to be called their God, for he has prepared a city for them. Hebrews 11:13-16

Do you feel like an alien when you find peace in a stressful situation? Feel love where there was once resentment or comfort where there should be pain? Do you feel trust during trials? Do you pray instead of crossing your fingers? We may not have green skin or computer chips in our heads, but all these things can make us feel or seem foreign to others. Be proud of your foreign/heavenly heritage. Take rest in knowing we will never be satisfied here. God has **set eternity in the hearts of men. Ecclesiastes 3:11**

Our hearts will always long for Heaven while we are here, but we have a loving God. I believe He offers us glimpses of eternal life and complete satisfaction. Wouldn't you agree that we get a little taste of Heaven when we hold a newborn baby, see the delight in a child's eyes or a beautiful sunset, or receive a hug from someone we love?

He has made everything beautiful in its time. He has also set eternity in the hearts of men; yet they cannot fathom what God has done from beginning to end. I know that there is nothing better for men than to be happy and do good while they live. Ecclesiastes 3:11-12

Relate – Can you relate to the message or theme? How? _____

_____

_____

_____

_____

_____

_____

Reread – Read the scriptures throughout today's message again.

_____

Revealed – Did God reveal anything new to you? Don't forget to come back and read them daily this week. God might not reveal to you today, but tomorrow.

_____

_____

_____

_____

_____

_____

Respond – Think about your week. Has God been whispering?

_____

_____

_____

_____

_____

_____

Reflect – Any other thoughts?

_____

_____

_____

_____

_____

_____

WEEK 31 ~ THE BOTTOM LINE

Scriptures: John 15:5, 1 Corinthians 9:24-27, Luke 10:41-42

Since I started writing these devotionals, my purpose has been to write what God teaches me through my life, circumstances and study. My hope is that you also will begin to notice Him at work in your life.

You know, God never changes. His lessons and messages have remained the same and He keeps His promises. The bottom line is the only thing that changes about God's Word is the people who teach or write about Him. Learning and studying the Word is imperative. What are the ways you continue to fill your mind and heart with His Word? Is it Bible study, church, Sunday school, small group, blog, devotional, conversations with friends or something else? All of these are great, but if you don't already take time alone with God and His word, I encourage you to do so. By listening only to others and not to Him, you are limiting what He can accomplish in and through you.

I am the vine; you are the branches. If a man remains in me and I in him, he will bear much fruit; apart from me you can do nothing. John 15:5

Take a scripture and pore over it, soak it in, pray over it, absorb it into your soul and ask God to reveal Himself to you. He will not let you down. When you are obedient and study His word, God is thrilled! He will bless you and show off for you in ways you never imagined. He will open your mind to things you never considered because when you serve God, you win!

Do you not know that in a race all the runners run, but only one gets the prize? Run in such a way as to get the prize. Everyone who competes in the games goes into strict training. They do it to get a crown that will not last; but we do it to get a crown that will last forever. Therefore I do not run like a man running aimlessly; I do not fight like a man beating the air. No, I beat my body and make it my slave so that after I have preached to others, I myself will not be disqualified for the prize. 1 Corinthians 9:24-27

So today I urge you to sit down with God's Word and listen for His whisper as He leads, reassures and encourages you. Today, for just 30 minutes, choose God over laundry, your favorite television show, chatting on the phone or running that one extra errand.

"Martha, Martha," the Lord answered, "you are worried and upset about many things, but only one thing is needed. Mary has chosen what is better, and it will not be taken away from her." Luke 10:41-42

Relate – Can you relate to the message or theme? How? _____

_____

_____

_____

_____

_____

_____

Reread – Read the scriptures throughout today's message again.

_____

Revealed – Did God reveal anything new to you? Don't forget to come back and read them daily this week. God might not reveal to you today, but tomorrow.

_____

_____

_____

_____

_____

_____

Respond – Think about your week. Has God been whispering?

_____

_____

_____

_____

_____

_____

Reflect – Any other thoughts?

_____

_____

_____

_____

_____

_____

WEEK 32 ~ INFOMERCIAL

Scriptures: Genesis 4:6-7, Isaiah 30:13, Psalm 89:26

My daughter came into the bathroom one morning to tell me all about a new cleaning product. She had even taken notes, and I quote, "hot, cool, nise (nice), stems (steams) floor, you can use it again and again. carpit glider." "Mommy, you would love this. It cleans germs off the floor," she expressed with delight. Ten minutes later, she was back in the bathroom telling me about a new exercise program. "I did these leg lifts about 30 times and look at how big my muscles already are!" she exclaimed. (No, we don't normally let our kids watch infomercials!)

Our children have innocent minds that believe what they hear and see. Although we as adults aren't so different from them. Like an infomercial, sin is waiting for us around every corner, just hoping we will have a weak moment, let our guard down and believe those lies inside our head. You aren't thin enough, you have earned it, you could do more, you aren't successful enough, they deserve it . . . Satan can fill our heads with lies that we will begin to believe if we aren't filling up our hearts and minds with God's Word and truths.

Why this tantrum? Why the sulking? If you do well, won't you be accepted? And if you don't do well, sin is lying in wait for you, ready to pounce; it's out to get you, you've got to master it. Genesis 4:6-7, The Message

How do we master our sin? How do we seal up the cracks around our hearts and minds so that sin can't creep in and crush us?

[T]his sin will become for you like a high wall, cracked and bulging, that collapses suddenly, in an instant. Isaiah 30:13

Fill your life with His Word, accept His blessings, praise Him in the storm, accept His direction, follow His path, allow His forgiveness to penetrate your heart and share His love with others. Jesus has to be our gatekeeper – the gatekeeper of our hearts and our minds. Allow Him entry and let Him take control.

He will call out to me, "You are my Father, my God, the Rock my Savior." Psalm 89:26

Relate – Can you relate to the message or theme? How? _____

_____

_____

_____

_____

_____

_____

Reread – Read the scriptures throughout today's message again.

_____

Revealed – Did God reveal anything new to you? Don't forget to come back and read them daily this week. God might not reveal to you today, but tomorrow.

_____

_____

_____

_____

_____

_____

Respond – Think about your week. Has God been whispering?

_____

_____

_____

_____

_____

_____

Reflect – Any other thoughts?

_____

_____

_____

_____

_____

_____

WEEK 33 ~ LOW BATTERY

Scriptures: Proverbs 17:19, Genesis 2:18, Ecclesiastes 4:10-12

We have one of those battery-operated ride-on cars. The kids love driving it around the yard and helping us do yardwork, but when the battery starts to run low it loses power and gets stuck much more frequently. I watched my two children ride together when we were out working in the yard one day. If the car got stuck in the leaves or grass, my son would get out to push and my daughter would press the gas pedal until they were moving again and he could jump back in.

It made me realize that as Christians our batteries run low sometimes. Our fire, hope, confidence and security in our Lord and Savior can diminish. We run low and forget the power and benefits of a full battery or a heart that runs completely with Christ. There are many reasons our battery can lose its charge: too busy to refuel, a challenging situation, an unanswered prayer or maybe a stronghold that is blocking our efforts to recharge.

Thank goodness we have friends, family, church members and strangers God places in our path who can give us a push back to full speed. Sometimes it is difficult to accept help when we need it, and sometimes we think we are too busy to offer help to someone who needs it, but alone we can be defeated. Don't build up walls, for **he who builds a high gate invites destruction. Proverbs 17:19** Hop out of your comfort zone and accept help from those who love you. God has said from the beginning in **Genesis 2:18, It's not good for the Man to be alone; I'll make him a helper, a companion.**

If one falls down,
his friend can help him up.
But pity the man who falls
and has no one to help him up!
Also, if two lie down together, they will keep warm.
But how can one keep warm alone?
Though one may be overpowered,
two can defend themselves.
A cord of three strands is not quickly broken. Ecclesiastes 4:10-12

Do you know someone who could use a little help recharging? Are you in need of some recharging, but haven't been willing to accept the help? Seek God in prayer today.

Relate – Can you relate to the message or theme? How? _____

_____

_____

_____

_____

_____

_____

Reread – Read the scriptures throughout today's message again.

_____

Revealed – Did God reveal anything new to you? Don't forget to come back and read them daily this week. God might not reveal to you today, but tomorrow.

_____

_____

_____

_____

_____

_____

Respond – Think about your week. Has God been whispering?

_____

_____

_____

_____

_____

_____

Reflect – Any other thoughts?

_____

_____

_____

_____

_____

_____

WEEK 34 ~ PRAYER

Scriptures: Philippians 4:12-13, 1 Peter 5:7, Psalm 119:71

"Prayer is like that she whispered, Sometimes it can take days . . . months . . . years and then sometimes when I get really quiet I can see, hear and feel the answer all at the same time."

A very dear friend of mine gave me a gorgeous print with this quote. I absolutely love it! It sums it all up for me. There are times when I pray and get an instant answer – and other prayers that seem to just sit out in space and take an eternity to be answered. Learning to enjoy the wait and be thankful for all the blessings I already have is the tricky part.

I know what it is to be in need, and I know what it is to have plenty. I have learned the secret of being content in any and every situation, whether well fed or hungry, whether living in plenty or in want. I can do everything through Him who gives me strength. Philippians 4:12-13

What a powerful scripture. In other words, Paul was saying, "Thank you for your prayers, help and concern. I really appreciate it, but you don't need to worry about me. I have found the recipe to being completely happy and satisfied no matter what my situation." Wow! Can you imagine saying that to someone? To be so content in resting in God's shadow and trusting no matter what the situation – knowing He will provide you the strength to get through and He is all you need. I think God allows needs in our lives so that we seek and depend on Him. It also gives Him the opportunity to show off for us and blow our minds with answered prayers we could have never imagined.

Cast all your anxiety on Him because He cares for you. 1 Peter 5:7

Think of a time (maybe it is happening right now) when your child was sick or a friend or family member was going through difficulties. How did you respond? You reached out, didn't you? And you wanted him or her to reach out to you, lean on you for help, support, love and advice.

Our Father in Heaven wants us to cast all our worries and problems on Him. He is there waiting. He wants to love on us, give us answers, comfort and peace. He wants to answer our prayers and teach us along the way so that each day we grow closer to being able to have contentment in every situation. **Philippians 4:12**

It was good for me to be afflicted so that I might learn your decrees. Psalms 119:71

Relate – Can you relate to the message or theme? How? _____

_____

_____

_____

_____

_____

Reread – Read the scriptures throughout today's message again.

_____

Revealed – Did God reveal anything new to you? Don't forget to come back and read them daily this week. God might not reveal to you today, but tomorrow.

_____

_____

_____

_____

_____

Respond – Think about your week. Has God been whispering?

_____

_____

_____

_____

_____

Reflect – Any other thoughts?

_____

_____

_____

_____

_____

WEEK 35 ~ CLING

Scriptures: Ezekiel 21:13, Hebrews 3:8, James 1:2-4, Psalm 63:7-8, Luke 8:1

When my daughter was little, we lost her "meow." The "meow" that helped her sleep at night, comforted her when she was sad and made nap time so much easier. Oh, it was a rough few days until we finally discovered where we had left it. When we lose something we need or care about, we search high, low and in every drawer. We will retrace our steps, call every store we have visited and double back to check every stop we made. But what if we lose something forever? Someone or something that can't be replaced: a marriage, a pet, a parent, a child or a dear friend? We still search high and low and retrace every step we made along the way, but we aren't looking for the person – we know he or she isn't there – we are searching for an answer.

We are searching for an answer, someone to blame or someone to be angry at, and a lot of times it is ourselves. For some reason, it makes us feel better or more in control if we can determine why or how something happened. We beg for answers: Why me, why them, why didn't I do more, why didn't I change? I should have . . . , I could have . . . .

God promises that **testing will surely come. Ezekiel 21:13** During times of loss or trials **do not harden your hearts Hebrews 3:8** for you are told that you should **consider it pure joy, my brothers, whenever you face trials of many kinds, because you know that the testing of your faith develops perseverance. James 1:2-4**

For me, that is a little difficult to swallow. Joy, really? That is a tall order. But we have a choice. We can shrivel up, hide, become bitter, consumed with guilt or we can cling to our Lord and Savior. Webster's defines cling as: 1a) to hold together 1b) to adhere as if glued firmly 1c) to hold or hold on tightly or tenaciously 2a) to have a strong emotional attachment or dependence 2b) to remain or linger as if resisting complete dissipation or dispersal.

Because you are my help, I sing in the shadow of your wings. My soul clings to you; your right hand upholds me. Psalm 63:7-8

This is exactly what I mean when I say cling to our Father in Heaven. We can't survive loss without him. We have to glue ourselves to Him because He will hold us up. Emotionally attach ourselves to Him and claim His promises, His peace and His Word. Do not let go! Remain with Him, for He is the only one who can stop our pain. The only one who can stop the "why" conversation in our head and the only one who can offer us complete peace. **Those on the rock are the ones who receive the word with joy when they hear it, but they have no root. They believe for a while, but in the time of testing they fall away. Luke 8:1**

Relate – Can you relate to the message or theme? How? _____

_____

_____

_____

_____

_____

_____

Reread – Read the scriptures throughout today's message again.

_____

Revealed – Did God reveal anything new to you? Don't forget to come back and read them daily this week. God might not reveal to you today, but tomorrow.

_____

_____

_____

_____

_____

_____

Respond – Think about your week. Has God been whispering?

_____

_____

_____

_____

_____

_____

Reflect – Any other thoughts?

_____

_____

_____

_____

_____

_____

WEEK 36 ~ GUTTER BALL

Scriptures: Ephesians 1:5-8, Psalm 68:19, Revelation 3:20

Our children were invited to a friend's birthday party at the bowling alley. The kids had so much fun, and the parents got a kick out of watching them try to navigate the ball down the alley. The bowling alley attendee assigned to our group was very attentive. She put bumpers in the gutters so the ball had no choice but to stay on the alley way and hit a pin or two. She even set up a contraption that rolls the ball for you if it's too heavy to swing. The kids were guaranteed a smile and the opportunity to knock down a few pins every time.

Our lives are just like that alley way. We try to stay on God's path – right down the center – but many times along the way we make a mistake or falter and end up in the gutter. I am just thankful that if we end up in the gutter with God we don't have to stay there to the end. When we repent, He will throw us back out there on the right path again. He forgives and forgives and He calls us to do the same. But how do we learn to stay out of the gutter? The more we fill up our gutters with God's Word, prayer and church, the less room there will be for us to misstep and fall into them. **In him we have redemption through his blood, the forgiveness of sins, in accordance with the riches of God's grace that He lavished on us with all wisdom and understanding. Ephesians 1:5-8**

And just like that special contraption that helps roll the ball down the alley, God is also there for us when things get too heavy and we feel like we don't have the energy for one more day. He lifts us up, points us in the right direction and helps us get started, but we have to turn to Him. We have to allow Him in, not turn Him away. We have to be obedient to His direction. It takes work and time and commitment, but the reward is great in this life and the next.

Blessed be the Lord – day after day he carries us along. He's our Savior, our God, oh yes! He's God-for-us, he's God-who-saves-us. Lord God knows all death's ins and outs. Psalm 68:19, The Message

Our God is for us – not against us! He is standing at the door of your heart waiting for you to allow Him in. Will you answer?

Here I am! I stand at the door and knock. If anyone hears my voice and opens the door, I will come in and eat with him, and he with me. Revelation 3:20

Relate – Can you relate to the message or theme? How? _____

_____

_____

_____

_____

_____

Reread – Read the scriptures throughout today's message again.

_____

Revealed – Did God reveal anything new to you? Don't forget to come back and read them daily this week. God might not reveal to you today, but tomorrow.

_____

_____

_____

_____

_____

Respond – Think about your week. Has God been whispering?

_____

_____

_____

_____

_____

Reflect – Any other thoughts?

_____

_____

_____

_____

_____

WEEK 37 ~ STUCK IN THE MUCK

Scriptures: Isaiah 38:17, Job 33:28, Psalm 40:2, Psalm 69:15

Surely it was for my benefit that I suffered such anguish. In your love you kept me from the pit of destruction; you have put all my sins behind your back. Isaiah 38:17

The word "pit" is mentioned many times in the Bible. It can mean abyss, chasm, hell, grave, tomb, well, hole, gorge. You get the picture. In the above scripture, depending on which translation you read, it means pit of death, pit of destruction, nothingness pit or rotting pit. It doesn't really sound like a place we would choose to go, but sometimes we do.

It is easy to fall into a pit of despair, self-pity, worry, fear or defeat, but we must pull ourselves out and **enjoy the light because God has redeemed us from going down to the pit. Job 33:28** Don't get me wrong, I have been in plenty of "pits" in my life. In fact, sometimes I just tell my friends, "I am in a pit today, but don't try to get me out. I am down here and I just want to stay for a day or two. I feel like having a drink and hanging up some wallpaper. In a few days I promise to come out." We all get a good laugh out of it, but telling them where I am is important because they will hold me accountable and check in on me to ensure I make an exit.

He lifted me out of the slimy pit, out of the mud and mire; he set my feet on a rock and gave me a firm place to stand. Psalm 40:2

Are you stuck in the muck? How long has it been? It may have only been a few days or it may have been for a while. You may have skipped the wallpaper to work on a full renovation. Make a decision today. Don't invest your time and energy in the "pit." Pray right now that your Father in Heaven will give you the strength and direction to pull yourself out. Tell a friend about your decision and ask him or her to check in on you to make sure you are staying on the right track.

I asked my son how he got to be so smart. "'Cause, my Daddy taught me," he replied. If we would just rely on our Heavenly Father, He will give us what we need to climb out and be with us every step of the way. He will teach us, direct us and guide us as we overcome the "pit" we have fallen into.

Do not let the floodwaters engulf me or the depths swallow me up or the pit close its mouth over me. Psalm 69:15

Relate – Can you relate to the message or theme? How? _____

_____

_____

_____

_____

_____

_____

Reread – Read the scriptures throughout today's message again.

_____

Revealed – Did God reveal anything new to you? Don't forget to come back and read them daily this week. God might not reveal to you today, but tomorrow.

_____

_____

_____

_____

_____

_____

Respond – Think about your week. Has God been whispering?

_____

_____

_____

_____

_____

_____

Reflect – Any other thoughts?

_____

_____

_____

_____

_____

_____

WEEK 38 ~ DOWNLOAD COMPLETE

Scriptures: 1 Chronicles 28:9, Psalm 63:1

I was explaining to my daughter that we didn't have a particular item she was requesting. "Can't you just get it from the Internet?" she pleaded. Oh, yes! My daughter, at only 6 years old, already understood and appreciated the wonders of technology. It is amazing. We can upgrade to a new version of software, order food, books, toys, music or anything else our hearts desire without even leaving our home.

However, there are still a few things we can't get from the Internet. We can't stick our finger in the computer and download a relationship with God. We can't order one either. It takes effort, study and discipline to get to know Him.

And you, my son Solomon, acknowledge the God of your father, and serve him with wholehearted devotion and with a willing mind, for the LORD searches every heart and understands every motive behind the thoughts. If you seek him, he will be found by you; but if you forsake him, he will reject you forever. 1 Chronicles 28:9

We have to find the time to spend with our Lord and Savior. Without His direction we will meander through life missing out on His plan, His opportunities and feeling the peace of His forgiveness. As I was putting my daughter to bed one night, she said, "Mommy, I love you so much. I can't even explain how much." That was such a special moment. As a mom, I crave to hear those words from my children. Especially as they get older.

It is the same with our Father in Heaven. He adores us! Hard to imagine with the way we act and the things we do sometimes, but He does. He desires time with us and wants us to seek and enjoy time alone with Him. He wants us to get to know Him through His Word, prayer and quiet time so that He can grow us in ways we never imagined. The more we know Him the more we trust Him, seek Him and are blessed by Him.

O God, you are my God, earnestly I seek you; my soul thirsts for you, my body longs for you, in a dry and weary land where there is no water. Psalm 63:1

Relate – Can you relate to the message or theme? How? _____

_____

_____

_____

_____

_____

_____

Reread – Read the scriptures throughout today's message again.

_____

Revealed – Did God reveal anything new to you? Don't forget to come back and read them daily this week. God might not reveal to you today, but tomorrow.

_____

_____

_____

_____

_____

_____

Respond – Think about your week. Has God been whispering?

_____

_____

_____

_____

_____

_____

Reflect – Any other thoughts?

_____

_____

_____

_____

_____

_____

WEEK 39 ~ HIDEOUT

Scriptures: James 4:8, Luke 9:18, Matthew 14:13, Luke 5:14, Mark 1:35, Jude 1:20

"Where is your Dad? I inquired. "Oh, he is working on his hideout," replied my daughter. Yes, it was true. My husband had spent several vacation days working on his new workshop. He was busy organizing, cleaning, designing and planning how he would hang his tools, store his equipment and organize everything efficiently to prevent clutter.

Webster's online dictionary defines a hideout as "a place of refuge, retreat, or concealment." I believe that as we continue to grow in our relationship with God, we should spend a little more time in our own "hideouts" planning, organizing and equipping ourselves with God's Word.

Come near to God and he will come near to you. Wash your hands, you sinners, and purify your hearts, you double-minded. James 4:8

We all need to make time to hide out with God. The benefits of doing so can be astonishing. There is no power, no peace, no strength and no love greater than His. Nothing and no one else can offer us what He has and desires to give us.

I often think about what Jesus did when He walked this earth. Surely, there is no better example for us to follow. Throughout the gospels we see examples of Jesus slipping away to "hide out" with God. When Jesus needed to recharge, receive direction, encouragement, strength or simply enjoy the presence of His Heavenly Father, he would simply slip away, withdraw or find a quiet spot alone.

One time when Jesus was off praying by himself Luke 9:18 When Jesus got the news, he slipped away by boat to an out-of-the-way place by himself. Matthew 14:13 As often as possible Jesus withdrew to out-of-the-way places for prayer. Luke 5:14 Very early in the morning, while it was still dark, Jesus got up, left the house and went off to a solitary place, where he prayed. Mark 1:35

Like Jesus, if we take some time to hide out with God we can draw our strength, direction and peace from Him. Fill your heart and mind with His Word, pray for His direction, discern His voice, watch for Him working in your life and praise His name every moment you get.

But you, dear friends, carefully build yourselves up in this most holy faith by praying in the Holy Spirit, staying right at the center of God's love, keeping your arms open and outstretched, ready for the mercy of our Master, Jesus Christ. This is the unending life, the real life! Jude 1:20

Relate – Can you relate to the message or theme? How? _____

_____
_____
_____
_____
_____
_____

Reread – Read the scriptures throughout today's message again.

_____

Revealed – Did God reveal anything new to you? Don't forget to come back and
read them daily this week. God might not reveal to you today, but tomorrow.

_____
_____
_____
_____
_____
_____

Respond – Think about your week. Has God been whispering?

_____
_____
_____
_____
_____
_____

Reflect – Any other thoughts?

_____
_____
_____
_____
_____
_____

WEEK 40 ~ CONTENTMENT

Scriptures: Isaiah 48:17, Psalm 37:7, Psalm 32:8, Matthew 9:29, 1 Peter 5:6-7

Our children were earning the privilege of opening an early Christmas present. It just so happened that our son was able to open his present a day before my daughter. She was so jealous. Not just about him getting to open the present early, but also about the gift he received. I heard it all – from "It's not fair!" to "He gets everything and I never get anything!" – until she opened her own gift and saw what she had been given. Then, the roles reversed and my son was jealous while my daughter was rejoicing. What a mess!

During my daughter's wait, I wanted to say so many things. "How can you say it isn't fair? You don't even know what you are getting! Just wait! Be patient, you will see your gift is just as great, if not more!"

This is what the LORD says – your Redeemer, the Holy One of Israel: "I am the LORD your God, who teaches you what is best for you, who directs you in the way you should go." Isaiah 48:17

Ah, patience . . . a virtue I am always working on. I was reminded of how often we go through this same ritual with God. Have you ever asked, "Why them and not me? Why me and not them? God, have you forgotten about me? This isn't fair." While all along God is whispering, be patient and remain in me for I have rewards for you that you can't even imagine. He wants to give us the desires of our heart, but we have to be still and trust in Him. **Psalm 37:7**

He is with us always and says, **I will instruct you and teach you in the way you should go; I will counsel you and watch over you. Psalm 32:8** Draw from His strength, love, compassion, grace and patience.

In **Matthew 9:29** Jesus says, **"According to your faith will it be done to you."** The closer we are to God, the more our faith grows. The more our faith grows, the more God can do for and through us. Trust Him and trust His timing. Be thankful for who you are and what God has provided for you today. Find contentment in who you are at this moment and find comfort in knowing that God is clearing a path just for you.

So be content with who you are, and don't put on airs. God's strong hand is on you; he'll promote you at the right time. Live carefree before God; he is most careful with you. 1 Peter 5:6-7, The Message

Relate – Can you relate to the message or theme? How? _____

_____

_____

_____

_____

_____

Reread – Read the scriptures throughout today's message again.

_____

Revealed – Did God reveal anything new to you? Don't forget to come back and read them daily this week. God might not reveal to you today, but tomorrow.

_____

_____

_____

_____

_____

_____

Respond – Think about your week. Has God been whispering?

_____

_____

_____

_____

_____

_____

Reflect – Any other thoughts?

_____

_____

_____

_____

_____

_____

WEEK 41 ~ JUST THAT SIMPLE

Scriptures: Deuteronomy 7:9, John 10:10, Isaiah 45:5, Isaiah 45:18

"Mommy, do you remember the Great Wolf Lodge?" my son asked. "Do you know why it is called that? Because it is GREAT, that's why!" he said emphatically.

Know therefore that the LORD your God is God; he is the faithful God, keeping his covenant of love to a thousand generations of those who love him and keep his commands. Deuteronomy 7:9

Sometimes, it is just that simple. We don't need to overanalyze, question or guess who our Lord and Savior is or what He promises. It is all in the name and written out for us in His Word. He is who He says He is. It is as simple as that if we will trust in Him.

Who is God?

He is Truth, Light, Everlasting, Love, Deliverer, Rock, Gentle Whisper, Almighty, the Great I Am, Prince of Peace, Ancient of Days, Abba, Comforter, King of Kings, Teacher, Alpha & Omega, Counselor, Creator, Judge . . . I wish I had more room to continue. I encourage you to research more of the names of God in the Bible. It is interesting, encouraging and important to understand and remember who God is. Soak it in dear friend because if we don't cover ourselves in these truths Satan will **come only to steal and kill and destroy John 10:10** those truths from your life, but he has no power over Christ.

I am the Lord, and there is none else; there is no God beside me. Isaiah 45:5

Just that simple. No need to question, **For this is what the LORD says — he who created the heavens, he is God; he who fashioned and made the earth, he founded it; he did not create it to be empty, but formed it to be inhabited— he says: "I am the LORD, and there is no other." Isaiah 45:18**

Lord, we thank You for all that You are. Please cover us in Your Word and help us understand and believe that You are who You say You are. Amen.

Relate – Can you relate to the message or theme? How? _____

_____

_____

_____

_____

_____

_____

Reread – Read the scriptures throughout today's message again.

_____

Revealed – Did God reveal anything new to you? Don't forget to come back and read them daily this week. God might not reveal to you today, but tomorrow.

_____

_____

_____

_____

_____

_____

Respond – Think about your week. Has God been whispering?

_____

_____

_____

_____

_____

_____

Reflect – Any other thoughts?

_____

_____

_____

_____

_____

_____

WEEK 42 ~ NO COINCIDENCE

Scriptures: Acts 17:24-25, Psalm 90:17, Psalm 19:1

You may or may not have experienced it. A time when you felt a nudge, intuition or persistent thought in the back of your head to send a card to a friend, make a phone call, drop off a meal or just stop in to say hello to a friend, neighbor or church member.

Or maybe a time when someone told you that God had placed you in their path, you said exactly what they needed to hear, you were an angel or an answer to prayer. Don't deny yourself the truth. We aren't that spectacular! We are nothing without God.

The God who made the world and everything in it is the Lord of heaven and earth and does not live in temples built by hands. And he is not served by human hands, as if he needed anything, because he himself gives all men life and breath and everything else. Acts 17:24-25

It wasn't a coincidence. It wasn't your idea, but it WAS God. Thankfully, you were open and obedient to his nudge so that He could use you to touch the life of another one of His children. This is something I pray about consistently. I pray that my heart and mind will be open to Him and his request – no matter how strange it may seem. I pray that my pride and self interests never interfere with His work and that I stay obedient to His Word.

There is nothing more humbling than to realize the Creator of the Universe has intervened and used you as a vessel to touch the life of one of His children. I am fortunate to have been the recipient of such encounters. I have also been blessed to have had the opportunity to be used by God to reach out to someone who has sought Him and His presence in their life.

May the favor of the Lord our God rest upon us; establish the work of our hands for us – yes, establish the work of our hands. Psalm 90:17

I pray you will receive this message with an accepting heart, open eyes and responsive soul to the requests God is whispering to you.

The heavens declare the glory of God; the skies proclaim the work of his hands. Psalm 19:1

Relate — Can you relate to the message or theme? How? _____

_____

_____

_____

_____

_____

Reread — Read the scriptures throughout today's message again.

_____

Revealed — Did God reveal anything new to you? Don't forget to come back and read them daily this week. God might not reveal to you today, but tomorrow.

_____

_____

_____

_____

_____

Respond — Think about your week. Has God been whispering?

_____

_____

_____

_____

_____

Reflect — Any other thoughts?

_____

_____

_____

_____

_____

WEEK 43 ~ HIS PRESENCE

Scriptures: Genesis 21:22, Hebrews 1:7, Psalm 139:7-10, Psalm 147:18

I can probably count on one hand the times in my life when I have truly felt the presence of the Lord. Emotionally, I feel His presence often, but physically it is very rare for me. One particular time stands out the most. In fact, I can always take myself there in my mind and relive it because it was so real.

When our daughter was 4 years old she had some medical issues arise. It all turned out fine, but it was a very difficult and scary time for us because we were unsure what the outcome would be. I had gone out early one morning with our dog. It was unusually cool that fall morning. I was enjoying a quiet moment when a gentle breeze swept up from behind and engulfed me. The breath of heaven blew in and wrapped around me. Tears began to well up in my eyes as I embraced and accepted this tremendous hug from the heavens. What an amazing reminder that **God is with us in everything we do. Genesis 21:22**

In speaking of the angels he says, "He makes his angels winds, his servants flames of fire." Hebrews 1:7

Oh, how I wish I could experience this every day. His physical presence brought an overwhelming sense of peace, love, satisfaction and stillness to my soul. I look forward to the day He offers Himself to me again in this way. I pray that my heart, mind and soul stay ready to receive it.

Where can I go from your Spirit? Where can I flee from your presence? If I go up to the heavens, you are there; if I make my bed in the depths, you are there. If I rise on the wings of the dawn, if I settle on the far side of the sea, even there your hand will guide me, your right hand will hold me fast. Psalm 139:7-10

I love soaking in His presence. I crave it, seek it and desire it. Do you crave His presence in your life? What inspires His presence? Is it a song, prayer, a beautiful setting, meditation, reading His Word, taking a quiet walk or something else? Stop now and pray for God to reveal Himself to you in a way He never has. I trust you will be greatly rewarded.

He sends his word and melts them; he stirs up his breezes, and the waters flow. Psalm 147:18

Relate – Can you relate to the message or theme? How? _____

_____

_____

_____

_____

_____

_____

Reread – Read the scriptures throughout today's message again.

_____

Revealed – Did God reveal anything new to you? Don't forget to come back and read them daily this week. God might not reveal to you today, but tomorrow.

_____

_____

_____

_____

_____

_____

Respond – Think about your week. Has God been whispering?

_____

_____

_____

_____

_____

_____

Reflect – Any other thoughts?

_____

_____

_____

_____

_____

_____

WEEK 44 ~ ALL THE PIECES

Scriptures: 2 Samuel 7:28, Deuteronomy 7:9, Jeremiah 39:17-18

My Dad recently lost his dog and his best friend. So, we had been talking a lot about life, death, God and heaven even more than usual on this particular weekend. I was getting my son ready for bed that evening, and he said, "Mommy, I am going to give you all the pieces of my life." "Really?!" I said. "What should I do with them?" With confidence and trust he replied, "Whatever you want to." Their sweet little thoughts continuously amaze me.

O Sovereign LORD, you are God! Your words are trustworthy, and you have promised these good things to your servant. 2 Samuel 7:28

Imagine if we were able to sit at the feet of our Lord and Savior and say, "Father, I give you all the pieces of my life." Can we say that to him and really mean it with all the faith and confidence in the world? We can't give him just a piece; we have to trust Him with all the pieces.

Every time I think I have done this successfully, I find another piece of my life that I am holding onto and trying to navigate alone. When I find myself struggling to find peace or an answer, I pause and realize that I have not given it to God.

Know therefore that the LORD your God is God; he is the faithful God, keeping his covenant of love to a thousand generations of those who love him and keep his commands. Deuteronomy 7:9

Today, take time to reflect on what pieces of your life you are still holding onto. Is it your job, marriage, work, family or some other challenge that you always have in the back of your mind? Locate it and hand it over today. Trust God to handle it. As my children say, "God knows everything!"

But I will rescue you on that day, declares the LORD; you will not be handed over to those you fear. I will save you; you will not fall by the sword but will escape with your life, because you trust in me, declares the LORD. Jeremiah 39:17-18

Relate – Can you relate to the message or theme? How? _____

_____

_____

_____

_____

_____

_____

Reread – Read the scriptures throughout today's message again.

_____

Revealed – Did God reveal anything new to you? Don't forget to come back and read them daily this week. God might not reveal to you today, but tomorrow.

_____

_____

_____

_____

_____

_____

Respond – Think about your week. Has God been whispering?

_____

_____

_____

_____

_____

_____

Reflect – Any other thoughts?

_____

_____

_____

_____

_____

_____

WEEK 45 ~ MILES TO GO

Scriptures: Psalm 9:10, Hebrews 12:11, Deuteronomy 32:4

On a recent family trip we got the usual, "Are we there yet?" and "How much longer?"

I think we use this approach when it comes to our relationship with God. We work toward a stronger relationship with Him but find we never complete the task. It can be discouraging. We find ourselves asking, "Are we there yet?" or "How much longer until I get it?"

A relationship with God is not a task we will ever be able to cross off our to-do list. It will not be completed in this lifetime, but we can't stop reaching for the goal because we will grow stagnant. **Those who know your name will trust in you, for you, LORD, have never forsaken those who seek you. Psalm 9:10**

If we stop growing in Christ, our lives will become like a swamp where the muck and mire of life start to sink our spirit and clog our judgment, goals, direction and relationships. No matter where you are in your walk with God, you are not finished yet and have miles to go.

After putting a Band-Aid on my son's finger one evening, he asked, "Why don't you ever get hurt?" I responded, "Oh, I do. It is just that I don't cry about the small stuff because I am old enough to know there are other things to cry about."

Life is filled with obstacles, challenges, pain, suffering, and you know the list goes on and on. I am sure you have experienced many of these trials yourself. But, if we continue to build our lives on Christ and His blessed hope, we can withstand the weight of this world. Don't give up on Him, don't stop studying His Word and don't push Him out of your life when things seem tough.

No discipline seems pleasant at the time, but painful. Later on, however, it produces a harvest of righteousness and peace for those who have been trained by it. Hebrews 12:11

No, we aren't there yet and we hopefully have a long way to go before our journey is complete. Attach yourself to God and the joys of life. Cling to love, laughter, joy, birth, good health, friendship and the many other blessings that this life can bring.

He is the Rock, his works are perfect, and all his ways are just. A faithful God who does no wrong, upright and just is he. Deuteronomy 32:4

Relate – Can you relate to the message or theme? How? _____

_____

_____

_____

_____

_____

_____

Reread – Read the scriptures throughout today's message again.

_____

Revealed – Did God reveal anything new to you? Don't forget to come back and read them daily this week. God might not reveal to you today, but tomorrow.

_____

_____

_____

_____

_____

_____

Respond – Think about your week. Has God been whispering?

_____

_____

_____

_____

_____

_____

Reflect – Any other thoughts?

_____

_____

_____

_____

_____

_____

WEEK 46 ~ WISDOM & STATURE

Scriptures: Luke 2:49-52, 2 John 1:4, Deuteronomy 4:5,9

After His birth, you don't hear much about Jesus until he is 12 and travels to Jerusalem for the Feast of the Passover and gets lost (or so His parents thought).

"Why were you searching for me?" he asked. "Didn't you know I had to be in my Father's house?" But they did not understand what he was saying to them. Then he went down to Nazareth with them and was obedient to them. But his mother treasured all these things in her heart. And Jesus grew in wisdom and stature, and in favor with God and men. Luke 2:49-52

I wish there were more stories in the Bible about Jesus when He was a little boy. I have so many questions. After Jesus broke a dish or drew on the walls, did Mary always remember He was the Son of God and handle the moment with patience and grace? Did she ever forget He was God's son and raise her voice in frustration? Or was Jesus, even as a child, God's perfect son and never ran into a moment when He required discipline?

I wonder why God left out the stories of Jesus' childhood. I would love to know what kind of parents Mary and Joseph were. Certainly they would be the greatest of role models when it came to parenting. Would their adventures in parenting put us all to shame or encourage us to strive to be the best parents we can be to our children? Even if our children are not the son or daughter of God, we are all His children.

It has given me great joy to find some of your children walking in the truth, just as the Father commanded us. 2 John 1:4

Because these stories were left out, we can only speculate about Jesus' life as a toddler and the parenting strategies that Mary and Joseph used. But we can look to the Bible for examples of what to teach our children. As parents, teachers or mentors, we should take the job seriously and strive to model Godly lives to the children around us so that they grow in wisdom and stature as Jesus did.

See, I have taught you decrees and laws as the LORD my God commanded me, so that you may follow them in the land you are entering to take possession of it. . . Only be careful, and watch yourselves closely so that you do not forget the things your eyes have seen or let them slip from your heart as long as you live. Teach them to your children and to their children after them. Deuteronomy 4:5, 9

Relate – Can you relate to the message or theme? How? _____

_____

_____

_____

_____

_____

_____

Reread – Read the scriptures throughout today's message again.

_____

Revealed – Did God reveal anything new to you? Don't forget to come back and read them daily this week. God might not reveal to you today, but tomorrow.

_____

_____

_____

_____

_____

_____

Respond – Think about your week. Has God been whispering?

_____

_____

_____

_____

_____

_____

Reflect – Any other thoughts?

_____

_____

_____

_____

_____

_____

WEEK 47 ~ BIG ENOUGH

Scriptures: Psalm 31:6, Isaiah 44:24, 26:2, 57:13, 51:8, Jeremiah 32:27

"Is God the biggest person in the world?" my son asked. "Yes." I responded. "So, he is small enough to live in our hearts and big enough to hold the whole world?" he replied.

This is what the LORD says – your Redeemer, who formed you in the womb: I am the LORD, who has made all things, who alone stretched out the heavens, who spread out the earth by myself. Isaiah 44:24

I could have never said it better. Oh, how children can make the most difficult seem simple. Yes, our God is enough. He is full of enough love, forgiveness and grace to fill our hearts and our lives so that it will flow over into those around us. The one who created the heavens, the earth and has placed the stars in the sky and knows them by name Genesis 1:16 loves you and me enough to dwell in us and to hold our cold, weary, misguided world in His hands. How I pray He never lets us go.

Don't be fooled by idols of power, money, healing or pleasure. They are powerless, **Isaiah 36:2** worthless, **Psalm 31:6** fragile **Isaiah 57:13** and will only bring shallow and temporary joy.

For the moth will eat them up like a garment; the worm will devour them like wool.
But my righteousness will last forever, my salvation through all generations. Isaiah 51:8

Focus instead on the one and only God, our Father in Heaven who sent His son through a virgin to live and die for us. He paid the ultimate sacrifice for you and for me. There should be no one above Him. You should give Him all praise. You should glorify His name and give thanks for His abundant and undeserved grace.

I am the LORD, the God of all mankind. Is anything too hard for me? Jeremiah 32:27

Relate – Can you relate to the message or theme? How? _____

_____

_____

_____

_____

_____

Reread – Read the scriptures throughout today's message again.

_____

Revealed – Did God reveal anything new to you? Don't forget to come back and read them daily this week. God might not reveal to you today, but tomorrow.

_____

_____

_____

_____

_____

Respond – Think about your week. Has God been whispering?

_____

_____

_____

_____

_____

Reflect – Any other thoughts?

_____

_____

_____

_____

_____

WEEK 48 ~ TREASURES

Scriptures: Matthew 6:19-20, 2 Timothy 1:13-14, Colossians 2:2-3

My children received an ant farm as a gift recently, and it's been so interesting to watch the gel turn from a solid substance into a maze of intricate tunnels and passages. The ants never seem to sleep. They just move quickly around, climbing over one another and taking pieces of gel to the top only to descend into the tunnels again to continue their work. They work night and day on creating their extensive and elaborate habitat only to die in one to three months. Then the instructions say you can simply rinse the dead ants out of the habitat they have created and keep it as a 3D form of art.

Do not store up for yourselves treasures on earth, where moth and rust destroy, and where thieves break in and steal. But store up for yourselves treasures in heaven, where moth and rust do not destroy, and where thieves do not break in and steal. Matthew 6:19-20

Like the ants, I think that many of us get caught up in the "now." We put more energy into the "I wants" and the earthly treasures than we do the heavenly ones. After all, don't we love instant gratification!? Our world caters to this desire. We have drive-through food, downloadable books, music and movies, Internet shopping, stores on every corner; and if we don't have the cash, we just charge it. We collect and acquire things our whole life only to leave them behind when we die.

What if we started thinking past this moment and this life? What if we placed our focus on the big picture – the eternal picture? Can you imagine how the world would change? It is almost impossible to conceive.

What you heard from me, keep as the pattern of sound teaching, with faith and love in Christ Jesus. Guard the good deposit that was entrusted to you – guard it with the help of the Holy Spirit who lives in us. 2 Timothy 1:13-14

Let's begin to focus on treasures that we can hold onto eternally and can never be taken from us. For the things that we hold close and guard within our hearts can't be taken from us.

My purpose is that they may be encouraged in heart and united in love, so that they may have the full riches of complete understanding, in order that they may know the mystery of God, namely, Christ, in whom are hidden all the treasures of wisdom and knowledge. Colossians 2:2-3

Relate – Can you relate to the message or theme? How? _____

_____

_____

_____

_____

_____

Reread – Read the scriptures throughout today's message again.

_____

Revealed – Did God reveal anything new to you? Don't forget to come back and read them daily this week. God might not reveal to you today, but tomorrow.

_____

_____

_____

_____

_____

Respond – Think about your week. Has God been whispering?

_____

_____

_____

_____

_____

Reflect – Any other thoughts?

_____

_____

_____

_____

_____

WEEK 49 ~ ALL I NEED

Scriptures: Colossians 2:6-7, Ephesians 3:12, Romans 8:35, Colossians 2:10, Luke 12:6-7

I picked up my daughter, put her in my lap and started hugging and kissing her. She said, "Ahhhh, this is what I need every second of the day. I have been trying to figure out what I need and this is it."

Do you ever have those days? Days when things seem just a little off-center, and you can't put your finger on what's wrong or what you need to balance things back out? There is only one solution, one way to bring your life back to center and put your feet firmly on the ground. Call upon our Lord and Savior, our friend.

My counsel for you is simple and straightforward: Just go ahead with what you've been given. You received Christ Jesus, the Master; now live him. You're deeply rooted in him. You're well constructed upon him. You know your way around the faith. Now do what you've been taught. School's out; quit studying the subject and start living it! And let your living spill over into thanksgiving. Colossians 2:6-7, *The Message*

He wants us to come to Him for all our needs and desires. **In him and through faith in him we may approach God with freedom and confidence. Ephesians 3:12** We can't be separated from Him. **Romans 8:35** He is waiting for you, waiting to give you all you need, waiting to fill the void you can't explain and make you complete in Him. **Colossians 2:10**

You don't have to search or wonder any longer. You are a child of God with access to His wisdom and love. Open the door and let Him in, crawl into His lap and allow Him to cover you with His love. He adores you.

Are not five sparrows sold for two pennies? Yet not one of them is forgotten by God. Indeed, the very hairs of your head are all numbered. Don't be afraid; you are worth more than many sparrows. Luke 12:6-7

Relate – Can you relate to the message or theme? How? _____

_____

_____

_____

_____

_____

_____

Reread – Read the scriptures throughout today's message again.

_____

Revealed – Did God reveal anything new to you? Don't forget to come back and read them daily this week. God might not reveal to you today, but tomorrow.

_____

_____

_____

_____

_____

_____

Respond – Think about your week. Has God been whispering?

_____

_____

_____

_____

_____

_____

Reflect – Any other thoughts?

_____

_____

_____

_____

_____

_____

WEEK 50 ~ UNCHARTED WATERS

Scriptures: Nehemiah 9:6, Psalm 25:4-8

Recently, I found myself in a strange situation. A situation I had never encountered in my life. Both of the strong, go-to people in my life where down. The two men in my life I've have always counted on to lift me up, keep things moving in a positive direction and just be there. They were both facing situations that were dragging them down and were barely able to keep their heads above the rough waters that seemed to be raging around them.

I was in uncharted waters and I felt completely inadequate to handle either situation. It was paralyzing. I felt so helpless. Just able to sit, watch and pray. That never feels like enough, does it? In the tough situations, we usually want to take action and fix the problem! Satan loves nothing more than for us to fall prey to these thoughts.

You alone are the LORD. You made the heavens, even the highest heavens, and all their starry host, the earth and all that is on it, the seas and all that is in them. You give life to everything, and the multitudes of heaven worship you. Nehemiah 9:6

It has been a terrific reminder that I am not in control and that I AM inadequate. God is the capable one. He alone. In fact, He does not even need my help. He may choose to enlist me in a certain situation, but He does not have to. He alone is Lord. Coming to terms with this can be difficult when you are watching those you love experience a confusing or painful time.

Show me your ways, O LORD, teach me your paths; guide me in your truth and teach me, for you are God my Savior, and my hope is in you all day long. Remember, O LORD, your great mercy and love, for they are from of old. Remember not the sins of my youth and my rebellious ways; according to your love remember me, for you are good, O LORD. Good and upright is the LORD; therefore he instructs sinners in his ways. Psalm 25:4-8

Let the following statements sink in as you read them.

God is enough. Our faith and hope should be in Him alone!

Prayer is enough! In fact, prayer is one of the most powerful tools God has given us.

Lean on Him and let Him take you through the uncharted waters of life. There is no better captain!

Relate – Can you relate to the message or theme? How? _____

_____

_____

_____

_____

_____

_____

Reread – Read the scriptures throughout today's message again.

_____

Revealed – Did God reveal anything new to you? Don't forget to come back and read them daily this week. God might not reveal to you today, but tomorrow.

_____

_____

_____

_____

_____

_____

Respond – Think about your week. Has God been whispering?

_____

_____

_____

_____

_____

_____

Reflect – Any other thoughts?

_____

_____

_____

_____

_____

_____

WEEK 51 ~ SHINE

Scriptures: John 1:1-5, Mark 4:19, Ezekiel 1:28, Genesis 9:15, John 1:5

In the beginning was the Word, and the Word was with God, and the Word was God. He was in the beginning with God. All things were made through him, and without him was not any thing made that was made. In him was life, and the life was the light of men. The light shines in the darkness, and the darkness has not overcome it. John 1:1-5

You know those days or even weeks when you find yourself worn out from it all, and good news seems like a train that left the station weeks ago and has yet to return? As I was driving the kids to school one morning, I was recounting (in my head) all the discouraging things that had been going on in my life and in the lives of those I love. So many times the **worries of this life, the deceitfulness of wealth and the desires for other things come in and choke the word, making it unfruitful. Mark 4:19**

As we topped a hill on Wade Avenue, I saw a little rainbow in the sky. It was sunny with just a few clouds that were heading out after an overnight storm, but there was a rainbow. The rays from the sunrise must have been hitting the clouds just right and there it was. My thoughts immediately turned from sadness to praise and I felt peace overcome me.

Like the appearance of a rainbow in the clouds on a rainy day, so was the radiance around him. This was the appearance of the likeness of the glory of the LORD. When I saw it, I fell facedown, and I heard the voice of one speaking. Ezekiel 1:28

God is our light on those dark days. He is the light that always shines in the darkness. Our God is so faithful and so tender. That rainbow was a beautiful reminder of His promises. Not just the promise that **never again will the waters become a flood to destroy all life, Genesis 9:15** but a promise of His love for us. He is always with us. He walks with us through fiery trials, He celebrates with us, He carries us when we can't take another step, He feels our pain and He counts our tears.

The next time clouds overtake you, look to the sky. Look to God and rely on His promises to carry you through. He is there for you and His light will always **shine through the darkness. John 1:5**

Relate – Can you relate to the message or theme? How? _____

_____

_____

_____

_____

_____

Reread – Read the scriptures throughout today's message again.

_____

Revealed – Did God reveal anything new to you? Don't forget to come back and read them daily this week. God might not reveal to you today, but tomorrow.

_____

_____

_____

_____

_____

Respond – Think about your week. Has God been whispering?

_____

_____

_____

_____

_____

Reflect – Any other thoughts?

_____

_____

_____

_____

_____

WEEK 52 ~ BOLD

Scriptures: Luke 11:8, Acts 4:31, Acts 28:31

We were back at school after a long vacation. Everyone was having a difficult time readjusting to our routine. We woke up on Tuesday morning running late, husband with a fever, kid's shoes muddy and we barely made it to school before the last bell rang.

Whew, I thought. I had dropped off one child and had one more to go before I could take a breath. From the backseat I hear, "Mommy, let's talk about Jesus Christ our Savior." (I'm not kidding! That is a direct quote.) Talk about a jolt back to reality. It was like someone shaking me and saying, "Get it together, girl. Focus on what's important."

His direct and very bold statement was refreshing and clear. I wonder how many times we miss the opportunity to be bold and direct with those around us? How many times we try to solve their problem(s) for them or offer our personal advice instead of pointing them in the direction of the ultimate solution – our Savior Jesus Christ.

I tell you, though he will not get up and give him the bread because he is his friend, yet because of the man's boldness he will get up and give him as much as he needs. Luke 11:8

It isn't easy to be bold with those around us. Sometimes, we know the correct direction to point them in [God's] but we choose not to. Are we embarrassed? Feel like it is the easy way out? Do we not think He is a good enough solution, or do we just forget He cares? I think the answer varies depending on the day, the situation and the person with whom we are talking.

After they prayed, the place where they were meeting was shaken. And they were all filled with the Holy Spirit and spoke the word of God boldly. Acts 4:31

Regardless of the circumstances, as Christians, it is imperative that we look up to the Lord and point others in His direction. Pray for Him to fill you with His Holy Spirit so that you have the courage, obedience and knowledge to speak boldly about His awesome and mysterious ways.

Boldly and without hindrance he preached the kingdom of God and taught about the Lord Jesus Christ. Acts 28:31

Relate – Can you relate to the message or theme? How? _____

_____

_____

_____

_____

_____

_____

Reread – Read the scriptures throughout today's message again.

_____

Revealed – Did God reveal anything new to you? Don't forget to come back and read them daily this week. God might not reveal to you today, but tomorrow.

_____

_____

_____

_____

_____

_____

Respond – Think about your week. Has God been whispering?

_____

_____

_____

_____

_____

_____

Reflect – Any other thoughts?

_____

_____

_____

_____

_____

_____

Your journey doesn't have to end here. Visit me on my blog at
www.thewhisperofgod.wordpress.com

I update it regularly with new thoughts and lessons that the Lord is using to
encourage and challenge me in my daily walk with Him.

**

*I pray that out of his glorious riches he may strengthen you with power through his
Spirit in your inner being, so that Christ may dwell in your hearts through faith. And I
pray that you, being rooted and established in love, may have power, together with all the
saints, to grasp how wide and long and high and deep is the love of Christ, and to
know this love that surpasses knowledge — that you may be filled to the measure of
all the fullness of God. Now to him who is able to do immeasurably more than all we
ask or imagine, according to his power that is at work within us, to him be glory in the
church and in Christ Jesus throughout all generations, forever and ever!
Amen. Ephesians 3:16-21*

~RESOURCES

www.biblegateway.com
www.biblestudytools.com
www.merriam-webster.com

QuickVerse Bible Suite Software, Standard Edition, 2010. www.quickverses.com

The New Strong's Concise Concordance & Vines Concise Dictionary of the Bible (Nashville, TN: Thomas Nelson, Inc. 1997, 1999).

Ken Anderson, *Where to Find it in the Bible,* (Nashville, TN: Thomas Nelson, Inc., 1996).

Emma & Culli Cain, my sweet children.

Kay Arthur, *Lord, Is It Warfare? Teach Me to Stand,* (WaterBrook Press, 1991), 186.

Beth Moore, lproof.org

Toby Mac, Portable Sound, *Lose My Soul, 2007*

Mike Lee, Senior Pastor, Hope Community Church, Cary, NC, www.gethope.net

Chanda Bell & Carol Aebersold, *The Elf on the Shelf, A Christmas Tradition,* 2007

Star Wars: The Clone Wars, Operation Huttlet, adapted by Steele Tyler Filipek, based on the movie *Star Wars: The Clone Wars,* 2008

~THANKS

The most important thing for you to know is that all the credit for this book goes to my Heavenly Father. He IS able to do immeasurably more than we can imagine. Ephesians 3:20 I am still in awe and humbled He would use this unworthy servant to spread His perfect Word.

I think my next thank you should go to my two wonderful children who have given me insight I once only dreamed about. Emma & Culli, you are two of the most wonderful, God-loving, smart people I know, and I love you dearly.

Matt, you are my best friend. I am so thankful and blessed to have you as a husband. Facing life every day is much easier knowing I have you as a partner. I love you.

I also have an expansive list of cheerleaders who have all helped me in their own special way.
Thank you to:

Mary Edna, for your prayers and encouragement, and pepper jelly.
Kelly, for direction, keeping me grounded and focused on the Lord's plan and not my own.
Mom, for being proud enough of my work to share it with your friends.
Daddy, for always believing I could anything in the world I chose to do.
Deborah, for warm toes and many prayers.
Jeannie, for your amazing editing skills and encouragement.
Women of the Dwell Bible study, for years of love, prayers and encouragement.
Scott, for all the publishing advice along the way. I highly recommend his book, *Holy IT!*
Passion Girls, for free therapy every month at girl's night out.
Ashley, for your gift of photography.
Kent Swecker, for coming to my rescue and creating a brilliant cover design.
And Mike Lee, you don't know it, but attending Hope and hearing your sermons has pushed me to a new level in my spiritual walk with my Lord and Savior. For this, I am forever grateful.

There are so many others. I am blessed to have such an amazing group of friends, family and prayer warriors. Thank you all!

Breinigsville, PA USA
12 May 2010
237873BV00004B/8/P